THE SCIENCE OF EDUCATION

First published 1878
This edition published by Lector House in 2024

ISBN: 978-93-6138-795-1

Lector House LLP
Registered Office: H. No. 96, Block C, Tomar Colony,
Burari, Delhi – 110084, India
info@lectorhouse.com
www.lectorhouse.com

THE SCIENCE OF EDUCATION

KARL ROSENKRANZ,
ANNA CALLENDER BRACKETT

2024

LECTOR HOUSE LLP

THE SCIENCE OF EDUCATION.

A Paraphrase of Dr. Karl Rosenkranz's Paedagogik Als System.

BY

ANNA C. BRACKETT.

PREFACE.

The translation of "Pedagogics as a System" was prepared and published five years ago. The wide demand for it that has made itself known since that time, especially in normal schools, has proved the value of such works in the domain of education. At the same time, the difficulty the students have always found in its use—a difficulty inseparable from any translation of a German metaphysical treatise—has led us to the conviction that a paraphrase into a more easily understood form is a necessity, if the thought of Rosenkranz is to be appropriated by the very class who are most in need of it. As was remarked in the preface to the translation, we have in English no other work of similar size which contains so much that is valuable to those engaged in the work of education. It is no compendium of rules or formulas, but rather a systematic, logical treatment of the subject, in which the attention is, as it were, concentrated upon the whole problem of education, while that problem is allowed to work itself out before us. To paraphrase the text—or, rather, to translate it from the metaphysical language in which it at present appears into a language more easy of comprehension—without losing the real significance of the statements, is the task which is here undertaken. Free illustrations and suggestions have been interwoven to give point and application to the thoughts and principles stated. This translation, or paraphrase, follows the paragraphs of the original and of the first translation. The analysis of the whole work, as it appeared in the original translation, is appended at the end of the "Introduction," as a guide to the student.

CONTENTS

INTRODUCTION.

§ 1. The science of Pedagogics may be called a secondary science, inasmuch as it derives its principles from others. In this respect it differs from Mathematics, which is independent. As it concerns the development of the human intelligence, it must wait upon Psychology for an understanding of that upon which it is to operate, and, as its means are to be sciences and arts, it must wait upon them for a knowledge of its materials. The science of Medicine, in like manner, is dependent on the sciences of Biology, Chemistry, Physics, etc. Moreover, as Medicine may have to deal with a healthy or unhealthy body, and may have it for its province to preserve or restore health, to assist a natural process (as in the case of a broken bone), or to destroy an unnatural one (as in the case of the removal of a tumor), the same variety of work is imposed upon Education.[1]

§ 2. Since the rules of Pedagogics must be extremely flexible, so that they may be adapted to the great variety of minds, and since an infinite variety of circumstances may arise in their application, we find, as we should expect, in all educational literature room for widely differing opinions and the wildest theories; these numerous theories, each of which may have a strong influence for a season, only to be overthrown and replaced by others.[2] It must be acknowledged that educational literature, as such, is not of a high order. It has its cant like religious literature. Many of its faults, however, are the result of honest effort, on the part of teachers, to remedy existing defects, and the authors are, therefore, not harshly to be blamed. It is also to be remembered that the habit of giving reproof and advice is one fastened

[1] The parallelism between these two sciences, Medicine and Education, is an obvious point, which every student will do well to consider.

[2] This will again remind the student of the theories of treatment in medicine in diseases which, in the seventeenth century, were treated only by bleeding and emetics, are now treated by nourishing food, and no medicines, etc.

in them by the daily necessity of their professional work.[3]

§ 3. As the position of the teacher has ceased to be undervalued, there has been an additional impetus given to self-glorification on his part, and this also—in connection with the fact that schools are no longer isolated as of old, but subject to constant comparison and competition—leads to much careless theorizing among its teachers, especially in the literary field.

§ 4. Pedagogics, because it deals with the human spirit, belongs, in a general classification of the sciences, to the philosophy of spirit, and in the philosophy of spirit it must be classified under the practical, and not the merely theoretical, division. For its problem is not merely to comprehend the nature of that with which it has to deal, the human spirit—its problem is not merely to influence one mind (that of the pupil) by another (that of the teacher)—but to influence it in such a way as to produce the mental freedom of the pupil. The problem is, therefore, not so much to obtain performed works as to excite mental activity. A creative process is required. The pupil is to be forced to go in certain beaten tracks, and yet he is to be so forced to go in these that he shall go of his own free will. All teaching which does not leave the mind of the pupil free is unworthy of the name. It is true that the teacher must understand the nature of mind, as he is to deal with mind, but when he has done this he has still his main principle of action unsolved; for the question is, knowing the nature of the mind, How shall he incite it to action, already predetermined in his own mind, without depriving the mind of the pupil of its own free action? How shall he restrain and guide, and yet not enslave?

If, in classifying all sciences, as suggested at the beginning of this section, we should subdivide the practical division of the Philosophy of Spirit, which might be called Ethics, one could find a place for Pedagogics under some one of the grades of Ethics. The education which the child receives through the influence of family life lies at the basis of all other teaching, and what the child learns of life, its duties, and possibilities, in its own home, forms the foundation for all after-work. On the life of the family, then, as a presupposition, all systems of Education must be built. In other words, the school must not attempt to initiate the child into the knowledge of the world—it must not assume the care of its first training;

[3] The teacher will do well to consider the probable result of the constant association with mental inferiors entailed by his work, and also to consider what counter-irritant is to be applied to balance, in his character, this unavoidable tendency.

that it must leave to the family.[4] But the science of Pedagogics does not, as a science, properly concern itself with the family education, or with that point of the child's life which is dominated by the family influence. That is education, in a certain sense, without doubt, but it does not properly belong to a science of Pedagogics. But, on the other hand, it must be remembered that this science, as here expounded, presupposes a previous family life in the human being with whom it has to deal.

§ 5. Education as a science will present the necessary and universal principles on which it is based; Education as an art will consist in the practical realization of these in the teacher's work in special places, under special circumstances, and with special pupils. In the skillful application of the principles of the science to the actual demands of the art lies the opportunity for the educator to prove himself a creative artist; and it is in the difficulty involved in this practical work that the interest and charm of the educator's work consists.

The teacher must thus adapt himself to the pupil. But, in doing so, he must have a care that he do not carry this adaptation to such a degree as to imply that the pupil is not to change; and he must see to it, also, that the pupil shall always be worked upon by the matter which he is considering, and not too much by the personal influence of the teacher through whom he receives it.[5]

§ 6. The utmost care is necessary lest experiments which have proved successful in certain cases should be generalized into rules, and a formal, dead creed, so to speak, should be adopted. All professional experiences are valuable as material on which to base new conclusions and to make new plans, but only for that use. Unless the day's work is, every day, a new creation, a fatal error has been made.

§ 7. Pedagogics as a science must consider Education—

(1) In its general idea;
(2) In its different phases;

[4] The age at which the child should be subject to the training of school life, or Education, properly so-called, must vary with different races, nations, and different children.

[5] The best educator is he who makes his pupils independent of himself. This implies on the teacher's part an ability to lose himself in his work, and a desire for the real growth of the pupil, independent of any personal fame of his own—a disinterestedness which places education on a level with the noblest occupations of man.

(3) In the special systems arising from this general idea, acting under special circumstances at special times.[6]

§ 8. With regard to the First Part, we remark that by Education, in its general idea, we do not mean any mere history of Pedagogics, nor can any history of Pedagogics be substituted for a systematic exposition of the underlying idea.

§ 9. The second division considers Education under three heads—as physical, intellectual, and moral—and forms, generally, the principal part of all pedagogical treatises.

In this part lies the greatest difficulty as to exact limitation. The ideas on these divisions are often undefined and apt to be confounded, and the detail of which they are capable is almost unlimited, for we might, under this head, speak of all kinds of special schools, such as those for war, art, mining, etc.

§ 10. In the Third Part we consider the different realizations of the one general idea of Pedagogics as it has developed itself under different circumstances and in different ages of the world.

The general idea is forced into different phases by the varying physical, intellectual, and moral conditions of men. The result is the different systems, as shown in the analysis. The general idea is one. The view of the end to be obtained determines in each case the actualization of this idea. Hence the different systems of Education are each determined by the stand-point from which the general ideal is viewed. Proceeding in this manner, it might be possible to construct a history of Pedagogics, *à priori*, without reference to actual history, since all the possible systems might be inferred from the possible definite number of points of view.

Each lower stand-point will lead to a higher, but it will not be lost in it. Thus, where Education, for the sake of the nation,[7] merges into the Education based on Christianity, the form is not thereby destroyed, but, rather, in the transition first attains its full realization. The systems of Education which were based on the idea of the nation had, in the fullness of time, outgrown their own limits, and needed a new form in order to contain their own true idea. The idea of the nation, as the highest principle, gives

[6] See analysis.

[7] Asiatic systems of Education have this basis (see § 178 of the original).

way for that of Christianity. A new life came to the old idea in what at first seemed to be its destruction. The idea of the nation was born again, and not destroyed, in Christianity.

§ 11. The final system, so far, is that of the present time, which thus is itself the fruit of all the past systems, as well as the seed of all systems that are to be. The science of Pedagogics, in the consideration of the system of the present, thus again finds embodied the general idea of education, and thus returns upon itself to the point from whence it set out. In the First and Second Parts there is already given the idea which dominates the system found thus necessarily existing in the present.

- Education
  - First Part. In its General Idea.
    - Its Nature.
    - Its Form.
    - Its Limits.
  - Second Part. In its Special Elements.
    - Physical.
    - Intellectual.
    - Moral.
  - Third Part. In its Particular Systems.
    - National.
      - Passive.
        - Family ... China.
        - Caste ... India.
        - Monkish ... Thibet.
      - Active.
        - Military ... Persia.
        - Priestly ... Egypt.
        - Industrial ... Phœnicia.
      - Individual.
        - Æsthetic ... Greece.
        - Practical ... Rome.
        - Abstract Individual ... Northern Barbarians.
    - Theocratic .... Jews.
    - Humanitarian.
      - Monkish.
      - Chivalric.
      - For Civil Life.
        - For Special Callings.
          - Jesuitic.
          - Pietistic.
        - To achieve an Ideal of Culture.
          - The Humanities.
          - The Philanthropic Movement.
        - For Free Citizenship.

FIRST PART.

THE GENERAL IDEA OF EDUCATION.

§ 12. A full treatment of Pedagogics must distinguish—

(1) The nature of Education;
(2) The form of Education;
(3) The limits of Education.

I. The Nature of Education.

§ 13. The nature of Education is determined by the nature of mind, the distinguishing mark of which is that it can be developed only from within, and by its own activity. Mind is essentially free—*i.e.*, it has the capacity for freedom—but it cannot be said to possess freedom till it has obtained it by its own voluntary effort. Till then it cannot be truly said to be free. Education consists in enabling a human being to take possession of, and to develop himself by, his own efforts, and the work of the educator cannot be said to be done in any sense where this is not accomplished. In general, we may say that the work of education consists in leading to a full development of all the inherent powers of the mind, and that its work is done when, in this way, the mind has attained perfect freedom, or the state in which alone it can be said to be truly itself.[8]

The isolated human being can never become truly man. If such human beings (like the wild girl of the forest of Ardennes) have been found,

[8] The definition of freedom here implied is this: Mind is free when it knows itself and wills its own laws.

they have only proved to us that reciprocal action with our fellow beings is necessary for the development of our powers. Caspar Hauser, in his subterranean prison, will serve as an example of what man would be without men. One might say that this fact is typified by the first cry of the newly-born child. It is as if the first expression of its seemingly independent life were a cry for help from others. On the side of nature the human being is at first quite helpless.

§ 14. Man is, therefore, the only proper object of education. It is true that we speak of the education of plants and of animals, but we instinctively apply other terms when we do so, for we say "raising" plants, and "training" animals. When we "train" or "break" an animal, it is true that we do, by pain or pleasure, lead him into an exercise of a new activity. But the difference between this and Education consists in the fact that, though he possessed capacity, yet by no amount of association with his kind would he ever have acquired this new development. It is as if we impress upon his plastic nature the imprint of our loftier nature, which imprint he takes mechanically, and does not himself recognize it as his own internal nature. We train him for our recognition, not for his own. But, on the contrary, when we educate a human being, we only excite him to create for himself, and out of himself, that for which he would most earnestly strive had he any appreciation of it beforehand, and in proportion as he does appreciate it he recognizes it joyfully as a part of himself, as his own inheritance, which he appropriates with a knowledge that it is his, or, rather, is a part of his own nature. He who speaks of "raising" human beings uses language which belongs only to the slave-dealer, to whom human beings are only cattle for labor, and whose property increases in value with the number.

Are there no school-rooms where Education has ceased to have any meaning, and where physical pain is made to produce its only possible result—a mechanical, external repetition? The school-rooms where the creative word—the only thing which can influence the mind—has ceased to be used as the means are only plantations, where human beings are degraded to the position of lower animals.

§ 15. When we speak of the Education of the human race, we mean the gradual growth of the nations of the earth, as a whole, towards the realization of self-conscious freedom. Divine Providence is the teacher here. The means by which the development is effected are the various circumstances and actions of the different races of men, and the pupils are the nations. The unfolding of this great Education is generally treated of under the head of Philosophy of History.

§ 16. Education, however, in a more restricted sense, has to do with the shaping of the individual. Each one of us is to be educated by the laws of physical nature—by the relations into which we come with the national life, in its laws, customs, etc., and by the circumstances which daily surround us. By the force of these we find our arbitrary will hemmed in, modified, and forced to take new channels and forms. We are too often unmindful of the power with which these forces are daily and hourly educating us—*i. e.*, calling out our possibilities into real existence. If we set up our will in opposition to either of these; if we act in opposition to the laws of nature; if we seriously offend the laws, or even the customs, of the people among whom we live; or if we despise our individual lot, we do so only to find ourselves crushed in the encounter. We only learn the impotence of the individual against these mighty powers; and that discovery is, of itself, a part of our education. It is sometimes only by such severe means that God is revealed to the man who persistently misunderstands and defies His creation. All suffering brought on ourselves by our own violation of laws, whether natural, ethical, or divine, must be, however, thus recognized as the richest blessing. We do not mean to say that it is never allowable for a man, in obedience to the highest laws of his spiritual being, to break away from the fetters of nature—to offend the ethical sense of his own people, or to struggle against the might of destiny. Reformers and martyrs would be examples of such, and our remarks above do not apply to them, but to the perverse, the frivolous, and the conceited; to those who are seeking in their action, not the undoubted will of God, but their own individual will or caprice.

§ 17. But we generally use the word Education in a still narrower sense than either of these, for we mean by it the working of one individual mind upon or within another in some definite and premeditated way, so as to fit the pupil for life generally, or for some special pursuit. For this end the educator must be relatively finished in his own education, and the pupil must possess confidence in him, or docility. He must be teachable. That the work be successful, demands the very highest degree of talent, knowledge, skill, and prudence; and any development is impossible if a well-founded authority be wanting in the educator, or docility on the part of the pupil.

Education, in this narrowest and technical sense, is an outgrowth of city or urban life. As long as men do not congregate in large cities, the three forces spoken of in § 16—*i.e.*, the forces of nature, national customs, and circumstances—will be left to perform most of the work of Education; but, in modern city life, the great complication of events, the uncertainty in the results—though careful forethought has been used—the immense development of individuality, and the pressing need of various information, break the power of custom, and render a different method necessary. The larger the city is, the more free is the individual in it from the restraints of customs, the less subjected to curious criticism, and the more able is he to give play to his own idiosyncrasies. This, however, is a freedom which needs the counterpoise of a more exact training in conventionalities, if we would not have it dangerous. Hence the rapid multiplication of educational institutions and systems in modern times (one chief characteristic of which is the development of urban life). The ideal Telemachus of Fenelon differs very much from the real Telemachus of history. Fenelon proposed an education which trained a youth to reflect, and to guide himself by reason. The Telemachus of the heroic age followed the customs ("use and wont") of his times with *naïve* obedience. The systems of Education once sufficient do not serve the needs of modern life, any more than the defenses once sufficient against hostile armies are sufficient against the new weapons adopted by modern warfare.

§ 18. The problem with which modern Education has to deal may be said, in general terms, to be the development in the individual soul of the indwelling Reason, both practical (as will) and theoretical (as intellect). To make a child good is only a part of Education; we have also to develop his intelligence. The sciences of Ethics and Education are not the same. Again, we must not forget that no pupil is simply a human being, like every other human being; he is also an individual, and thus differs from every other one of the race. This is a point which must never be lost sight of by the educator. Human beings may be—nay, must be—educated in company, but they cannot be educated simply in the mass.

§ 19. Education is to lead the pupil by a graded series of exercises, previously arranged and prescribed by the educator, to a definite end. But these exercises must take on a peculiar form for each particular pupil under the special circumstances present. Hasty and inconsiderate work *may*, by chance, accomplish much; but no work which is not *systematic* can advance and fashion him in conformity with his tenure, and such alone is to be called Education; for Education implies both a comprehension of the end to be attained and of the means necessary to compass that end.

§ 20. Culture, however, means more and more every year; and, as the sum total of knowledge increases for mankind, it becomes necessary, in order to be a master in any one line, to devote one's self almost exclusively to that. Hence arises, for the teacher, the difficulty of preserving the unity and wholeness which are essential to a complete man. The principle of division of labor comes in. He who is a teacher by profession becomes one-sided in his views; and, as teaching divides and subdivides into specialities, this abnormal one-sideness tends more and more to appear. Here we find a parallelism in the profession of Medicine, with a corresponding danger of narrowness; for that, too, is in a process of constant specialization, and the physician who treats nervous diseases is likely to be of the opinion that all trouble arises from that part of the organism, or, at least, that all remedies should be applied there. This tendency to one-sideness is inseparable from the progress of civilization and that of science and arts. It contains, nevertheless, a danger of which no teacher should be unwarned. An illustration is furnished by the microscope or telescope; a higher power of the instrument implies a narrower field of view. To concentrate our observation upon one point implies the shutting out of others. This difficulty with the teacher creates one for the pupil.

In this view one might be inclined to judge that the life of the savage as compared with that of civilized man, or that of a member of a rural community as compared with that of an inhabitant of a city, were the more to be desired. The savage has his hut, his family, his cocoa-palm, his weapons, his passions; he fishes, hunts, amuses himself, adorns himself, and enjoys the consciousness that he is the center of a little world; while the denizen of a city must often acknowledge that he is, so to speak, only one wheel of a gigantic machine. Is the life of the savage, therefore, more favorable to human development? The characteristic idea of modern civilization is: The development of the individual as the end for which the State exists. The great empires of Persia, Egypt, and India, wherein the individual was of value only as he ministered to the strength of the State, have given way to the modern nations, where individual freedom is pushed so far that the State seems only an instrument for the good of the individual. From being the supreme end of the individual, the State has become the means for his advancement into freedom; and with this very exaltation of the value of the mere individual over the State, as such, there is inseparably connected the seeming destruction of the wholeness of the individual man. But the union of State and individual, which was in ancient times merely mechanical, has now become a living process, in which constant interaction gives rise to all the intellectual life of modern civilization.

§ 21. The work of Education being thus necessarily split up, we have the distinction between general and special schools. The work of the former is to give general development—what is considered essential for all men; that of the latter, to prepare for special callings. The former should furnish a basis for the latter—*i.e.*, the College should precede the Medical School, etc., and the High School the Normal. In the United States, owing to many causes, this is unfortunately not the case.

The difference between city and country life is important here. The teacher in a country school, and, still more, the private tutor or governess, must be able to teach many more things than the teacher in a graded school in the city, or the professor in a college or university. The danger on the one side is of superficiality, on the other of narrowness.

§ 22. The Education of any individual can be only relatively finished. His possibilities are infinite. His actual realization of those possibilities must always remain far behind. The latter can only approximate to the former. It can never reach them. The term "finishing an education" needs, therefore, some definition; for, as a technical term, it has undoubtedly a meaning. An immortal soul can never complete its development; for, in so doing, it would give the lie to its own nature. We cannot speak properly, however, of educating an idiot. Such an unfortunate has no power of generalization, and no conscious personality. We can train him mechanically, but we cannot educate him. This will help to illustrate the difference, spoken of in § 14, between Education and Mechanical training.

We obtain astonishing results, it is true, in our schools for idiots, and yet we cannot fail to perceive that, after all, we have only an external result. We produce a mechanical performance of duties, and yet there seems to be no actual mental growth. It is an exogenous, and not an endogenous, growth, to use the language of Botany.[9] Continual repetition, under the most gentle patience, renders the movements easy, but, after all, they are only automatic,

[9] Perhaps, however slow the growth, there is real progress in liberating the imprisoned

or what the physicians call reflex.

We have the same result produced in a less degree when we attempt to teach an intelligent child something which is beyond his active comprehension. A child may be taught to do or say almost anything by patient training, but, if what he is to say is beyond the power of his mental comprehension, and hence of his active assimilation, we are only training him as we train an animal (§ 14), and not educating him. We call such recitations parrot recitations, and, by our use of the word, express exactly in what position the pupils are placed. An idiot is only a case of permanently arrested development. What in the intelligent child is a passing phase is for the idiot a fixed state. We have idiots of all grades, as we have children of all ages.

The above observations must not be taken to mean that children should never be taught to perform operations in arithmetic which they do not, in cant phrase, "perfectly understand," or to learn poetry whose whole meaning they cannot fathom. Into this error many teachers have fallen.

There can be no more profitable study for a teacher than to visit one of these numerous idiot schools. He finds the alphabet of his professional work there. As the philologist learns of the formation and growth of language by examining, not the perfectly formed languages, but the dialects of savage tribes, so with the teacher. In like manner more insight into the philosophy of teaching and of the nature of the mind can be acquired by teaching a class of children to read than in any other grade of work.

II. The Form of Education.

§ 23. The general form of Education follows from the nature of mind. Mind is nothing but what it itself creates out of its own activity. It is, at first, mind as undeveloped or unconscious (in the main); but, secondly, it acquires the power of examining its own action, of considering itself as an object of attention, as if it were a quite foreign thing—*i.e.*, it reflects (in this stage it is really ignorant that it is studying its own nature); and, finally, it becomes conscious that this, which it had been examining, and of whose existence it is conscious, is its own self: It attains self-consciousness. It is through this

soul (?)

estrangement from itself, given back to itself again and restored to unity, but it is no longer a simple, unconscious unity. In this third state only can it be said to be free—*i.e.*, to possess itself. Education cannot create; it can only help to develop into reality the previously-existent possibility; it can only help to bring forth to light the hidden life.

§ 24. All culture, in whatever line, must pass through these two stages of estrangement and of reunion; the reunion being not of two different things, but the recognition of itself by thought, and its acceptance of itself as itself. And the more complete is the estrangement—*i.e.*, the more perfectly can the thought be made to view itself as a somewhat entirely foreign to itself, to look upon it as a different and independent somewhat—the more complete and perfect will be its union with and acceptance of its object as one with itself when the recognition does finally take place. Through culture we are led to this conscious possession of our own thought. Plato gives to the feeling, with which knowledge must necessarily begin, the name of wonder. But wonder is not knowledge; it is only the first step towards it. It is the half-terrified attention which the mind fixes on an object, and the half-terror would be impossible did it not dimly forebode that it was something of its own nature at which it was looking. The child delights in stories of the far-off, the strange, and the wonderful. It is as if they hoped to find in these some solution to themselves—a solution which they have, as it were, asked in vain of familiar scenes and objects. Their craving for such is the proof of how far their nature transcends all its known conditions. They are like adventurous explorers who push out to unknown regions in hopes of finding the freedom and wealth which lies only within themselves. They want to be told about things which they never saw, such as terrible conflagrations, banditti life, wild animals, gray old ruins, Robinson Crusoes on far-off, happy islands. They are irresistibly attracted by whatever is highly colored and dazzlingly lighted. The child prefers the story of Sinbad the Sailor to any tales of his own home and nation, because mind has this necessity of getting, as it were, outside of itself so as to obtain a view of itself. As the child grows to youth he is, from the same reasons, desirous of traveling.

§ 25. Work may be defined as the activity of the mind in a conscious concentration on, and absorption in, some object, with the purpose of acquiring or producing it. Play is the activity of the mind which gives itself up to surrounding objects according to its own caprice, without any thought as to results. The Educator gives out work to the pupil, but he leaves him to himself in his play.

§ 26. It is necessary to draw a sharp line between work and play. If the Educator has not respect for work as an activity of great weight and importance, he not only spoils the relish of the pupil for play, which loses all its charm of freedom when not set off by its antithesis of earnest labor, but he undermines in the pupil's mind all respect for any real existence. On the other hand, he who does not give to the child space, time, and opportunity for play prevents the originality of his pupil from free development through the exercise of his creative ingenuity. Play sends the child back to his work refreshed, because in it he loses himself without constraint and according to his own fancy, while in work he is required to yield himself up in a manner prescribed for him by another.

Let the teacher watch his pupils while at play if he would discover their individual peculiarities, for it is then that they unconsciously betray their real propensities. This antithesis of work and play runs through the entire life, the form only of play varying with years and occupations. To do what we please, as we please, and when we please, not for any reason, but just because we please, remains play always. Children in their sports like nothing better than to counterfeit what is to be the earnest work of their after-lives. The little girl plays with her dolls, and the boy plays he is a soldier and goes to mimic wars.

It is, of course, an error to suppose that the play of a child is simply muscular. The lamb and the colt find their full enjoyment in capering aimlessly about the field. But to the child play would be incomplete which did not bring the mind into action. Children derive little enjoyment from purely muscular exercise. They must at the same time have an object requiring mental action to attain it. A number of children set simply to run up and down a field would tire of the exercise in five minutes; but put a ball amongst them and set them to a game and they will be amused by it for hours.

Exceptional mental development is always preceded, and is, indeed, produced by, an exceptional amount of exercise in the form of play on the part of the special faculties concerned. The peculiar tendencies exhibited in play are due to the large development of particular faculties, and the ultimate giant strength of a faculty is brought about by play. The genius is no doubt born, not made; but, although born, it would dwindle away in infancy were it not for the constant exercise taken in play, which is as necessary for development as food for the maintenance of life.

§ 27. Work should never be treated as if it were play, nor play as if it were work. Those whose work is creative activity of the mind may find recreation in the details of science; and those, again, whose vocation is scientific research can find recreation in the practice of art in its different departments. What is work to one may thus be play to another. This does not, however, contradict the first statement.

§ 28. It is the province of education so to accustom us to different conditions or ways of thinking and acting that they shall no longer seem strange or foreign to us. When these have become, as we say, "natural" to us—when we find the acquired mode of thinking or acting just what our inclination leads us to adopt unconsciously, a *Habit* has been formed. A habit is, then, the identity of natural inclination with the special demands of any particular doing or suffering, and it is thus the external condition of all progress. As long as we require the conscious act of our will to the performance of a deed, that deed is somewhat foreign to ourselves, and not yet a part of ourselves. The practical work of the educator may thus be said to consist in leading the mind of the pupil over certain lines of thought till it becomes "natural" or spontaneous for him to go by that road. Much time is wasted in schools where the pupil's mind is not led aright at first, for then he has to unlearn habits of thought which are already formed. The work of the teacher is to impress good methods of studying and thinking upon the minds of his pupils, rather than to communicate knowledge.

§ 29. It is, at first sight, entirely indifferent what a Habit shall relate to—*i.e.*, the point is to get the pupil into the way of forming habits, and it is not at first of so much moment what habit is formed as that a habit is formed. But we cannot consider that there is anything morally neutral in the abstract, but only in the concrete, or in particular examples. An action may be of no moral significance to one man, and under certain circumstances, while to another man, or to the same man under different circumstances, it may have quite a different significance, or may possess an entirely opposite character. Appeal must be made, then, to the individual conscience of each one to decide what is and what is not permissible to that individual under the given circumstances. Education must make it its first aim to awaken in the pupil a sensitiveness to spiritual and ethical distinctions which knows that nothing is in its own nature morally insignificant or indifferent, but shall recognize, even in things seemingly small, a universal human significance. But, yet, in relation to the highest interests of morality or the well-being of society, the pupil must be taught to subordinate without hesitation all that relates exclusively to his own personal comfort or welfare for the well-being of his fellow-men, or for moral rectitude.

When we reflect upon habit, it at once assumes for us the character of useful or injurious. The consequences of a habit are not indifferent.

Whatever action tends as a harmonious means to the realization of our purpose is desirable or advantageous, and whatever either partially contradicts or wholly destroys it is disadvantageous. Advantage and disadvantage being, then, only relative terms, dependent upon the aim or purpose which we happen to have in view, a habit which may be advantageous to one man under certain circumstances may be disadvantageous to another man, or even to the same man, under other circumstances. Education must, then, accustom the youth to consider for himself the expediency or inexpediency of any action in relation to his own vocation in life. He must not form habits which will be inexpedient with regard to that.

§ 31. There is, however, an *absolute* distinction of habits as morally good and bad. From this absolute stand-point we must, after all, decide what is for us allowable or forbidden, what is expedient and what inexpedient.

§ 32. As to its form, habit may be either passive or active. By passive habit is meant a habit of composure which surveys undisturbed whatever vicissitudes, either external or internal, may fall to our lot, and maintains itself superior to them all, never allowing its power of acting to be paralyzed by them. It is not, however, merely a stoical indifference, nor is it the composure which comes from inability to receive impressions—a sort of impassivity. It is that composure which is the highest result of power. Nor is it a selfish love of ease which intentionally withdraws itself from annoyances in order to remain undisturbed. It is not manifested because of a desire to be out of these vicissitudes. It is, while in them, to be not of them. It is the composure which does not fret itself over what it cannot change. The soul that has built for itself this stronghold of freedom within itself may vividly experience joy and sorrow, pain and pleasure, and yet serenely know that it is intrenched in walls which are inaccessible to their attacks, because it knows that it is infinitely superior to all that may chance or change. What is meant by active habit in distinction from passive habit is found in our external activity, as skill, facility, readiness of information, etc. It might be considered as the equipping of our inner selves for active contest with the external world; while passive habit is the fortifying of our inner selves against the attack of the external world. The man who possesses habit in both these forms impresses himself in many different ways on the outer world, while at the same time, and all the time, he preserves intact his personality from the constant assaults of the outer world. He handles both spear and shield.

§ 33. All education, in whatever line, must work by forming habits physical, mental, or moral. It might be said to consist in a conversion of actions which are at first voluntary, by means of repetition, into instructive actions which are performed, as we say, naturally—*i.e.*, without any conscious volition. We teach a child to walk, or he teaches himself to walk by a constant repetition of the action of the will upon the necessary muscles; and, when the thinking brain hands over the mechanism to the trained spinal cord, the anxious, watchful look disappears from the face, and the child talks or laughs as he runs: then that part of his education is completed. Henceforth the attention that had been necessary to manage the body in walking is freed for other work. This is only an illustration, easily understood, of what takes place in all education. Mental and moral acts, thoughts, and feelings in the same way are, by repetition, converted into habits and become our nature; and character, good or bad, is only the aggregate of our habits. When we say a person has no character, we mean exactly this: that he has no fixed habits. But, as the great end of human life is freedom, he must be above even habit. He must not be wholly a machine of habits, and education must enable him to attain the power of breaking as well as of forming habits, so that he may, when desirable, substitute one habit for another. For habits may be (§ 29), according to their nature, proper or improper, advantageous or disadvantageous, good or bad; and, according to their form, may be (§ 32) either the acceptance of the external by the internal or the reaction of the internal upon the external. Through our freedom we must be able, not only to renounce any habit formed, but to form a new and better one. Man should be supreme above all habits, wearing them as garments which the soul puts on and off at will. It must so order them all as to secure for itself a constant progress of development into still greater freedom. In this higher view habits become thus to our sight only necessary accompaniments of imperfect freedom. Can we conceive of God, who is perfect Freedom, as having any habits? We might say that, as a means toward the ever-more decided realization of the Good, we must form a habit of voluntarily making and breaking off habits. We must characterize as bad those habits which relate only to our personal convenience or enjoyment. They are often not essentially blameworthy, but there lies in them a hidden danger that they may allure us into luxury or effeminacy. It is a false and mechanical way of looking at the affair to suppose that a habit which had been formed by a certain number of repetitions can be broken off by an equal number of refusals. We can never utterly renounce a habit which we decide to be undesirable for us except through decision and firmness.

§ 34. Education, then, must consider the preparation for authority and obedience (§ 17); for a rational ordering of one's actions according to universal principles, and, at the same time, a preservation of individuality (§ 18); for work and play (§ 25); for habits of spontaneity or originality (§ 28). To endeavor by any set rules to harmonize in the pupil these opposites will be a vain endeavor, and failure in the solution of the problem is quite possible by reason of the freedom of the pupil, of surrounding circumstances, or of mistakes on the part of the teacher, and the possibility of this negative result must, therefore, enter as an element of calculation into the work itself. All the dangers which may in any way threaten the youth must be considered in advance, and he must be fortified against them. While we should not intentionally expose the youth to temptation in order to prove his strength of resistance, neither should we, on the other hand, endeavor to seclude him from all chance of dangerous temptation. To do the former would be satanic; while to do the latter would be ridiculous, useless, and in fact dangerous in the highest degree, for temptation comes more from within than from without, and any secret inclination will in some way seek, or even create, its own opportunity for gratification. The real safety from sin lies, not in seclusion of one's self from the world[10]—for all the elements of worldliness are innate in each individual—but in an occupying of the restless activity in other ways, in learning and discipline; these being varied as time goes on, according to the age and degree of proficiency. Not to crush out, but to direct, the child's activity, whether physical or mental, is the key to all real success in education. The sentimentalism which has, during the last few years, in this country (the United States), tended to diminish to so great an extent the actual work to be performed by our boys and girls, has set free a dangerous amount of energy whose new direction gives cause for grave alarm. To endeavor to prevent the youth from all free and individual relations with the

[10] "When me they fly, I am the wings."—*Emerson.*

real world, implies a never-ending watch kept over him. The consciousness of being thus "shadowed" destroys in the youth all elasticity of spirit, all confidence, and all originality. A constant feeling of, as it were, a detective police at his side obscures all sense of independent action, systematically accustoming him to dependence. Though, as the tragic-comic story of Peter Schlemihl shows, the loss of a man's own shadow may involve him in a series of fatalities,[11] yet to be "shadowed" constantly by a companion, as in the pedagogical system of the Jesuits, undermines all naturalness. And, if we endeavor to guard too strictly against what is evil and wrong, the pupil reacts, bringing all his intelligence into the service of his craft and cunning, till the would-be educator stands aghast at the discovery of such evil-doing as he had supposed impossible under his strict supervision. Within the circle of whatever rules it may be found necessary to draw around the young there must always be left space for freedom. Pupils should always be led to see that all rules against which they fret are only of their own creation; and that as grave-stones mark the place where some one has fallen, so every law is only a record of some previous wrong-doing. The law "Thou shalt not kill" was not given till murder had been committed. In other words, the wrong deed preceded the law against it, and perfect obedience is the same as perfect freedom. No obedience except that which we gain from the pupil's own convictions has real educational significance.

§ 35. If there appears in the youth any decided deformity opposed to the ideal which we would create in him, we should at once inquire into its history and origin. The negative and positive are so closely related, and depend so intimately on each other, in our being that what appears to us to be negligence, rudeness, immorality, foolishness, or oddity may arise from some real necessity of the pupil which in its process of development has only taken a wrong direction.

§ 36. If it should appear, on such examination, that the wrong action was the result of avoidable ignorance, of caprice, or willfulness on the part of the pupil, this calls for a simple prohibition on the part of the teacher, no reason being assigned. His authority must be sufficient for the pupil without any reason. When the fault is repeated, and the pupil is old enough to understand, then only should the grounds of the prohibition be stated with it. This should, however, be done in few words, and the educator must never allow himself to lose, in a doctrinal lecture, the idea of discipline. If he do,

[11] The story of Peter Schlemihl, by Chamisso, may be read in the English translation published in "Hedge's German Prose Writers."

the pupil will soon forget that it was his own misbehavior which was the cause of all the remarks. The statement of the reason must be honest, and must be presented to the youth on the side most easy for him to appreciate. False reasons are not only morally wrong, but they lead the mind astray. We also commit a grave error when we try to unfold to the youth all the possible consequences of his wrong act, for those possible consequences are too far off to affect his mind. The long lecture wearies him, especially if it be in a stereotyped form; and with teachers who are fault-finding, and who like to hear themselves talk, this is apt to be the case. Still more unfortunate would it be if we really should affect the lively imagination of a sensitive youth by our description of the wretchedness to which his wrong-doing, if persisted in, might lead him, for then the conviction that he has already taken one step in that direction may produce in him a fear which in the future man may become terrible depression and lead to degradation.

§ 37. If to censure we add the threat of punishment, we have then what in common language is called scolding.

If threats are made, the pupil must be made to feel that they will be faithfully executed according to the word.

The threat of punishment is, however, to be avoided; for circumstances may arise which will render its fulfillment not only objectionable, but wrong, and the teacher will then find himself in the position of Herod and bound "for his oath's sake" to a course of action which no longer seems the best. Even the law in affixing a penalty to definite crimes allows a certain latitude in a maximum and minimum of awarded punishment.

§ 38. It is only after other means of reformation have been tried, and have failed, that punishment is justifiable for error, transgression, or vice. When our simple prohibition (§ 36), the statement of our reason for the prohibition (§ 36), and threat of punishment (§ 37) have all failed, then punishment comes and intentionally inflicts pain on the youth in order to force him by this last means to a realization of his wrong-doing. And here the punishment must not be given for general bad conduct or for a perverse disposition—those being vague generalities—but for a special act of wrong-doing at that time. He should not be punished because he is naturally bad or because he is generally naughty, but for this one special and particular act which he has committed. Thus the punishment will act on the general disposition, not directly, but through this particular act, as a manifestation of the disposition. Then it will not accuse the innermost nature of the culprit. This way of punishment is not only demanded by justice, but it is absolutely necessary in view of the fact of the sophistry inherent in human nature which is always busy in assigning various motives for its actions. If the child understands, then, that he is punished for that particular act which he knows himself to have committed, he cannot feel the bitter sense of injustice and misunderstanding which a punishment inflicted for general reasons, and which attributes to him a depravity of motives and intentions, so often engenders.

§ 39. Punishment as an educational means must, nevertheless, be always essentially corrective, since it seeks always to bring the youth to a comprehension of his wrong-doing and to a positive alteration in his behavior, and, hence, has for its aim to improve him. At the same time it is a sad testimony of the insufficiency of the means which have been previously tried. We should on no account aim to terrify the youth by physical force, so that to avoid that he will refrain from doing the wrong or from repeating a wrong act already done. This would lead only to terrorism, and his growing strength would soon put him beyond its power and leave him without motive for refraining from evil. Punishment may have this effect in some degree, but it should, above all, be made to impress deeply upon his mind the eternal truth that the evil deed is never allowed in God's universe to act unrestrained and according to its own will, but that the good and true is the only absolute power in the world, and that it is never at a loss to avenge any contradiction of its will and design.

It may be questioned whether the moral teaching in our schools be not too negative in its measures; whether it do not confine itself too much to forbidding the commission of the wrong deed, and spend too little force in securing the performance of the right deed. Not a simple refraining from the wrong, but an active doing of the right would be the better lesson to inculcate.

In the laws of the state the office of punishment is first to satisfy justice,[12] and only after this is done can the improvement of the criminal be considered. If government should proceed on the same basis as the educator, it would make a grave mistake, for it has to deal, not with children, but with adults, to whom it concedes the dignity of full responsibility for all their acts. It has not to consider the reasons, either psychological or ethical,

[12] That is, punishment is retributive and not corrective. Justice requires that each

which prompted the deed. The actual deed is what it has first of all to deal with, and only after that is considered and settled can it take into view any mitigating circumstances connected therewith, or any peculiarity of the individual. The educator, on the other hand, has to deal with those who are immature and only growing toward responsibility. As long as they are under the care of a teacher, he is at any rate partially accountable for what they do. We must never confound the nature of punishment in the State with that of punishment as an educational means.

§ 40. As to punishment, as with all other work in education, it can never be abstractly determined beforehand, but it must be regulated with a view to the individual pupil and his peculiar circumstances. What it shall be, and how and when administered, are problems which call for great ingenuity and tact on the part of the educator. It must never be forgotten that punishments vary in intensity at the will of the educator. He fixes the standard by which they are measured in the child's mind. Whipping is actual physical pain, and an evil in itself to the child. But there are many other punishments which involve no physical pain, and the intensity of which, as felt by the child, varies according to an artificial standard in different schools. "To sit under the clock" was a great punishment in one of our public schools—not that the seat was not perfectly comfortable, but that one was never sent there to sit unless for some grave misdemeanor. The teacher has the matter in his own hands, and it is well to remember this and to grade his punishments with much caution, so as to make all pass for their full value. In some schools even suspension is so common that it does not seem to the pupil a very terrible thing. "Familiarity breeds contempt," and frequency implies familiarity. A punishment seldom resorted to will always seem to the pupil to be severe. As we weaken, and in fact bankrupt, language by an inordinate use of superlatives, so, also, do we weaken any punishment by its frequent repetition. Economy of resources should be always practiced.

---

man shall have the fruits of his own deeds; in this it assumes that each and every man is free and self-determined. It proposes to treat each man as free, and as the rightful owner of his deed and its consequences. If he does a deed which is destructive to human rights, it shall destroy his rights and deprive him of property, personal freedom, or even of life. But corrective punishment assumes immaturity of development and consequent lack of freedom. It belongs to the period of nurture, and not to the period of maturity. The tendency in our schools is, however, to displace the forms of mere corrective punishment (corporal chastisement), and to substitute for them forms founded on retribution—*e.g.*, deprivation of privileges. See secs. 42 and 43.

§ 41. In general, we might say that, for very young children, corporal punishment is most appropriate; for boys and girls, isolation; and for older youth, something which appeals to the sense of honor.

§ 42. (1) Corporal punishment implies physical pain. Generally it consists of a whipping, and this is perfectly justifiable in case of persistent defiance of authority, of obstinate carelessness, or of malicious evil-doing, so long or so often as the higher perceptions of the offender are closed against appeal. But it must not be administered too often, or with undue severity. To resort to deprivation of food is cruel. But, while we condemn the false view of seeing in the rod the only panacea for all embarrassing questions of discipline on the teacher's part, we can have no sympathy for the sentimentality which assumes that the dignity of humanity is affected by a blow given to a child. It is wrong thus to confound self-conscious humanity with child-humanity, for to the average child himself a blow is the most natural form of retribution, and that in which all other efforts at influence at last end. The fully grown man ought, certainly, not to be flogged, for this kind of punishment places him on a level with the child; or, where it is barbarously inflicted, reduces him to the level of the brute, and thus absolutely does degrade him. In English schools the rod is said to be often used; if a pupil of the first class, who is never flogged, is put back into the second, he becomes again subject to flogging. But, even if this be necessary in the schools, it certainly has no proper place in the army and navy.

§ 43. (2) To punish a pupil by isolation is to remove him temporarily from the society of his fellows. The boy or girl thus cut off from companionship, and forced to think only of himself, begins to understand how helpless he is in such a position. Time passes wearily, and he is soon eager to return to the companionship of parents, brothers and sisters, teachers and fellow-students.

But to leave a child entirely by himself without any supervision, and perhaps in a dark room, is as wrong as to leave two or three together without supervision. It often happens when they are kept after school by themselves that they give the freest rein to their childish wantonness, and commit the wildest pranks.

§ 44. (3) Shutting children up in this way does not touch their sense of honor, and the punishment is soon forgotten, because it relates only to certain particular phases of their behavior. But it is quite different when the pupil is isolated from his fellows on the ground that by his conduct he has violated the very principles which make civilized society possible, and is, therefore, no longer a proper member of it. This is a punishment which touches his sense of honor, for honor is the recognition of the individual by others as their equal, and by his error, or by his crime, he had forfeited his right to be their equal, their peer, and has thus severed himself from them.

The separation from them is thus only the external form of the real separation which he himself has brought to pass within his soul, and which his wrong-doing has only made clearly visible. This kind of punishment, thus touching the whole character of the youth and not easily forgotten, should be administered with the greatest caution lest a permanent loss of self-respect follow. When we think our wrong-doing to be eternal in its effects, we lose all power of effort for our own improvement.

This sense of honor cannot be developed so well in family life, because in the family the ties of blood make all in a certain sense equal, no matter what may be their conduct. He who has by wrong-doing severed himself from society is still a member of the family, and within its sacred circle is still beloved, though it may be with bitter tears. No matter how wrong he may have been, he still can find there the deepest sympathy, for he is still father, brother, etc. It is in the contact of one family with another that the feeling of honor is first developed, and still more in the contact of the individual with an institution which is not bound to him by any natural ties, but is an organism entirely external to him. Thus, to the child, the school and the school-classes offer a means of development which can never be found in the family.

This fact is often overlooked by those who have the charge of the education of children. No home education, no private tutorship, can take the place of the school as an educational influence. For the first time in his life the child, on being sent to school, finds himself in a community where he is responsible for his own deeds, and where he has no one to shield him. The rights of others for whom he has no special affection are to be respected by him, and his own are to be defended. The knowledge gained at the school is by no means the most valuable acquisition there obtained. It must never be forgotten by the teacher that the school is an institution on an entirely different basis from the family, and that personal attachment is not the principle on which its rule can be rightly based.

§ 45. This gradation of punishment from physical pain, up through occasional isolation, to the touching of the innermost sense of honor is very carefully to be considered, both with regard to the different ages at which they are severally appropriate and to the different discipline which they necessarily produce. Every punishment must, however, be always looked at as a means to some end, and is thus transitory in its nature. The pupil should always be conscious that it is painful to the teacher to punish him. Nothing can be more effectual as a means of cure for the wrong-doer than to perceive in the manner and tone of the voice, in the very delay with which the necessary punishment is administered, that he who punishes also suffers in order that the wrong-doer may be cured of his fault. The principle of vicarious suffering lies at the root of all spiritual healing.

III. The Limits of Education.

§ 46. As far as the external form of education is concerned, its limit is reached in the instrumentality of punishment in which we seek to turn the activity which has been employed in a wrong direction into its proper channel, to make the deed positive instead of negative, to substitute for the destructive deed one which shall be in harmony with the constructive forces of society. But education implies its real limits in its definition, which is to build up the individual into theoretical and practical Reason. When this work goes properly on, the authority of the educator, as authority, necessarily loses, every day, some of its force, as the guiding principles come to form a part of the pupil's own character, instead of being superimposed on him from without through the mediation of the educator. What was authority becomes now advice and example; unreasoning and implicit obedience passes into gratitude and affection. The pupil wears off the rough edges of his crude individuality, which is transfigured, so to speak, into the universality and necessity of Reason, but without losing his identity in the process. Work becomes enjoyment, and Play is found only in a change of activity. The youth takes possession of himself, and may now be left to himself. There are two widely differing views with regard to the limits of education; one lays great stress on the powerlessness of the pupil and the great power of the teacher, and asserts that the teacher must create something out of the pupil.

This view is often seen to have undesirable results, where large numbers are to be educated together. It assumes that each pupil is only "a sample of the lot" on whom the teacher is to affix his stamp, as if they were different pieces of goods from some factory. Thus individuality is destroyed, and all reduced to one level, as in cloisters, barracks, and orphan asylums, where only one individual seems to exist. Sometimes it takes the form of a theory which holds that one can at will flog anything into or out of a pupil. This may be called a superstitious belief in the power of education. The opposite extreme may be found in that system which advocates a "severe letting alone," asserting that individuality is unconquerable, and that often the most careful and circumspect education fails of reaching its aim because the inherent nature of the youth has fought against it with such force as to render abortive all opposing efforts. This idea of Pedagogy produces a sort of indifference about means and ends which would leave each individuality to grow as its own instinct and the chance influences of the world might direct. The latter view would, of course, preclude the possibility of any science of education, and make the youth only the sport of blind fate. The comparative power of inherited tendencies and of educational appliances is, however, one which every educator should carefully study. Much careless generalization has been made on this topic, and opinion is too often based upon some one instance where accurate observation of methods and influences have been wanting.

§ 47. Education has necessarily a definite *subjective limit* in the individuality of the youth, for it can develop in him only that which exists in him as a possibility. It can lead and assist, but it has no power to create. What nature has denied to a man education cannot give him, any more than it can on the other hand annihilate his original gifts, though it may suppress, distort, and measurably destroy them. And yet it is impossible to decide what is the real essence of a man's individuality until he has left behind him the years of growth, because it is not till then that he fully attains conscious possession of himself. Moreover, at this critical time many traits which were supposed to be characteristic may prove themselves not to be so by disappearing, while long-slumbering and unsuspected talents may crop out. Whatever has been forced upon a child, though not in harmony with his individuality, whatever has been driven into him without having been actively accepted by him, or having had a definite relation to his culture—will remain perhaps, but only as an external foreign ornament, only as a parasitic growth which weakens the force of his real nature. But we must distinguish from these little affectations which arise from a misconception of the limits of individuality that effort of imitation which children and young people often exhibit in trying to copy in their own actions those peculiarities which they observe and admire in perfectly-developed persons with whom they may come in contact. They see a reality which corresponds to their own possibility, and the presentiment of a like or a similar attainment stirs them to imitation, although this external imitation may be sometimes disagreeable or ridiculous to the lookers-on. We ought not to censure it too severely, remembering that it springs from a positive striving towards true culture, and needs only to be properly directed, and never to be roughly put down.

§ 48. *The objective limit* of education consists in the means which can be applied for it. That the capacity for culture should exist is the first condition of success, but it is none the less necessary that it be cultivated. But how much cultivation shall be given to it must depend in very great degree on the means which are practicable, and this will undoubtedly again depend on the worldly possessions and character of the family to which the pupil belongs. If he comes of a cultivated and refined family, he will have a great advantage at the start over his less favored comrades; and, with regard to many of the arts and sciences, this limitation of education is of great significance. But the means alone will not answer. Without natural capacity, all the educational apparatus possible is of no avail. On the other hand, real talent often accomplishes incredible feats with very limited means; and, if the way is only once open, makes of itself a center of attraction which draws to itself as with magnetic power the necessary means. Moral culture is, however, from its very nature, raised above such dependence.

If we fix our thought on the subjective limit—that of individuality (§ 47)—we detect the ground for that indifference which lays little stress on education (§ 46, end). If, on the other hand, we concentrate our attention on the means of culture, we shall perceive the reason of the other extreme spoken of—of that pedagogical despotism (§ 46) which fancies that it is able to prescribe and enforce at will upon the pupil any culture whatever, without regard to his special characteristics.

§ 49. Education comes to its *absolute limit* when the pupil has apprehended the problem which he is to solve, has comprehended the means which are at his disposal, and has acquired the necessary skill in using them. The true educator seeks to render himself unnecessary by the complete emancipation of the youth. He works always towards the independence of the pupil, and always with the design of withdrawing so soon as he shall have reached this stand-point, and of leaving him to the full responsibility for his own deeds. To endeavor to hold him in the position of a pupil after this time has been reached would be to contradict the very essence of education, which must find its result in the independent maturity of the youth. The inequality which formerly existed between pupil and teacher is now removed, and nothing becomes more oppressive to the former than any endeavor to force upon him the authority from which, in reality, his own efforts have freed him. But the undue hastening of this emancipation is as bad an error as an effort after delay. The question as to whether a person is really ready for independent action—as to whether his education is finished—may be settled in much the same way in education as in politics. When any people has progressed so far as to put the question whether they are ready for freedom, it ceases to be a question; for, without the inner consciousness of freedom itself, the question would never have occurred to them.

§ 50. But, although the pupil may rightly now be freed from the hands of instructors, and no longer obtain his culture through them, it is by no means to be understood that he is not to go on with the work himself. He is now to educate himself. Each must plan out for himself the ideal toward which he must daily strive. In this process of self-transformation a friend may aid by advice and example, but he cannot educate, for the act of educating necessarily implies inequality between teacher and pupil. The human necessity for companionship gives rise to societies of different kinds, in which we may, perhaps, say that there is some approach to educating their members, the necessary inequality being supplied by various grades and orders. They presuppose education in the usual sense of the word, but they wish to bring about an education in a higher sense, and, therefore, they veil the last form of their ideal in mystery and secrecy.

By the term *Philister* the Germans indicate the man of a civilized state who lives on, contented with himself and devoid of any impulse towards further self-culture. To one who is always aspiring after an Ideal, such a one cannot but be repulsive. But how many are they who do not, sooner or later, in mature life, crystallize, as it were, so that any active life, any new progress, is to them impossible?

ANALYSIS AND COMMENTARY.

§ 1. Pedagogics is not a complete, independent science by itself. It borrows the results of other sciences [*e.g.*, it presupposes the science of Rights, treating of the institutions of the family and civil society, as well as of the State; it presupposes the science of anthropology, in which is treated the relations of the human mind to nature. Nature conditions the development of the individual human being. But the history of the individual and the history of the race presents a continual emancipation from nature, and a continual growth into freedom, *i.e.*, into ability to know himself and to realize himself in the world by making the matter and forces of the world his instruments and tools. Anthropology shows us how man as a natural being—*i.e.*, as having a body—is limited. There is climate, involving heat and cold and moisture, the seasons of the year, etc.; there is organic growth, involving birth, growth, reproduction, and decay; there is race, involving the limitations of heredity; there is the telluric life of the planet and the circulation of the forces of the solar system, whence arise the processes of sleeping, waking, dreaming, and kindred phenomena; there is the emotional nature of man, involving his feelings, passions, instincts, and desires; then there are the five senses, and their conditions. Then, there is the science of phenomenology, treating of the steps by which mind rises from the stage of mere feeling and sense-perception to that of self-consciousness, *i.e.*, to a recognition of mind as true substance, and of matter as mere phenomenon created by Mind (God). Then, there is psychology, including the treatment of the stages of activity of mind, as so-called "faculties" of the mind, *e.g.*, attention, sense-perception, imagination, conception, understanding, judgment, reason, and the like. Psychology is generally made (by English writers) to include, also, what is here called anthropology and phenomenology. After psychology, there is the science of ethics, or of morals and customs; then, the Science of Rights, already mentioned; then, Theology, or the Science of Religion, and, after all these, there is Philosophy, or the Science of Science. Now, it is clear that the Science of Education treats of the process of development, by and through which man, as a merely natural being, becomes spirit, or self-conscious mind; hence, it presupposes all the sciences named, and will be defective if it ignores nature, or mind, or any stage or process of either, especially Anthropology, Phenomenology, Psychology, Ethics, Rights, Æsthetics, or Science of Art and Literature, Religion, or Philosophy].

§ 2. The scope of pedagogics being so broad, and its presuppositions so vast, its limits are not well defined, and its treatises are very apt to lack logical sequence and conclusion; and, indeed, frequently to be mere collections of unjustified and unexplained assumptions, dogmatically set forth. Hence the low repute of pedagogical literature as a whole.

§ 3. Moreover, education furnishes a special vocation, that of teaching. (All vocations are specializing—being cut off, as it were, from the total life of man. The "division of labor" requires that each individual shall concentrate his endeavors and be a *part* of the whole).

§ 4. Pedagogics, as a special science, belongs to the collection of sciences (already described, in commenting on § 1) included under the philosophy of Spirit or Mind, and more particularly to that part of it which relates to the will (ethics and science of rights, rather than to the part relating to the intellect and feeling, as anthropology, phenomenology, psychology, æsthetics, and religion. "Theoretical" relates to the *intellect*, "practical" relates to the *will*, in this philosophy). The province of practical philosophy is the investigation of the nature of freedom, and the process of securing it by self-emancipation from nature. Pedagogics involves the conscious exertion of influence on the part of the will of the teacher upon the will of the pupil, with a purpose in view—that of inducing the pupil to form certain prescribed habits, and adopt prescribed views and inclinations. The entire science of mind (as above shown), is presupposed by the science of education, and must be kept constantly in view as a guiding light. The institution of the *family* (treated in practical philosophy) is the starting-point of education, and without this institution properly realized, education would find no solid foundation. The right to be educated on the part of children, and the duty to educate on the part of parents, are reciprocal; and there is no family life so poor and rudimentary that it does not furnish the most important elements of education—no matter what the subsequent influence of the school, the vocation, and the state.

§ 5. Pedagogics as science, distinguished from the same as an art: the former containing the abstract general treatment, and the latter taking into consideration all the conditions of concrete individuality, *e.g.*, the peculiarities of the teacher and the pupil, and all the local circumstances, and the power of adaptation known as "tact."

§ 6. The special conditions and peculiarities, considered in education as an art, may be formulated and reduced to system, but they should not be introduced as a part of the *science* of education.

§ 7. Pedagogics has three parts: first, it considers the idea and nature of education, and arrives at its true definition; second, it presents and describes the special provinces into which the entire field of education is divided; third, it considers the historical evolution of education by the human race, and the individual systems of education that have arisen, flourished, and decayed, and their special functions in the life of man.

§ 8. The scope of the first part is easy to define. The history of pedagogics, of course, contains all the ideas or definitions of the nature of education; but it must not for that reason be substituted for the scientific investigation of the nature of education, which alone should constitute this first part (and the history of education be reserved for the third part).

§ 9. The second part includes a discussion of the threefold nature of man as body, intellect, and will. The difficulty in this part of the science is very great, because of its dependence upon other sciences (*e.g.*, upon physiology, anthropology, etc.), and because of the temptation to go into details (*e.g.*, in the practical department, to consider the endless varieties of schools for arts and trades).

§ 10. The third part contains the exposition of the various national standpoints furnished (in the history of the world) for the bases of particular systems of education. In each of these systems will be found the general idea underlying all education, but it will be found existing under special modifications, which have arisen through its application to the physical, intellectual, and ethical conditions of the people. But we can deduce the essential features of the different systems that may appear in history, for there are only a limited number of systems possible. Each lower form finds itself complemented in some higher form, and its function and purpose then become manifest. The systems of "national" education (*i.e.*, Asiatic systems, in which the individuality of each person is swallowed up in the substantiality of the national idea—just as the individual waves get lost in the ocean on whose surface they arise) find their complete explanation in the systems of education that arise in Christianity (the preservation of human life being the object of the nation, it follows that when realized abstractly or exclusively, it absorbs and annuls the mental independence of its subjects, and thus contradicts itself by destroying the essence of what it undertakes to preserve, *i.e.*, life (soul, mind); but within Christianity the principle of the state is found so modified that it is consistent with the infinite, untrammelled development of the individual, intellectually and morally, and thus not only life is saved, but spiritual, free life is attainable for each and for all).

§ 11. The history of pedagogy ends with the present system as the latest one. As science sees the future ideally contained in the present, it is bound to comprehend the latest system as a realization (though imperfect) of the ideal system of education. Hence, the system, as scientifically treated in the first part of our work, is the system with which the third part of our work ends.

§ 12. The nature of education, its form, its limits, are now to be investigated. (§§ 13-50.)

§ 13. The nature of education determined by the nature of Mind or Spirit, whose activity is always devoted to realizing for itself what it is potentially—to becoming conscious of its possibilities, and to getting them under the control of its will. Mind is potentially free. Education is the means by which man seeks to realize in man his possibilities (to develop the possibilities of the race in each individual). Hence, education has freedom for its object.

§ 14. Man is the only being capable of education, in the sense above defined, because the only conscious being. He must know himself ideally, and then realize his ideal self, in order to become actually free. The animals not the plants may be *trained*, or *cultivated*, but, as devoid of self-consciousness (even the highest animals not getting above impressions, not reaching ideas, not seizing general or abstract thoughts), they are not realized for *themselves*, but only for us. (That is, they do not know their ideal as we do.)

§ 15. Education, taken in its widest compass, is the education of the human race by Divine Providence.

§ 16. In a narrower sense, education is applied to the shaping of the individual, so that his caprice and arbitrariness shall give place to rational habits and views, in harmony with nature and ethical customs. He must not abuse nature, nor slight the ethical code of his people, nor despise the gifts of Providence (whether for weal or woe), unless he is willing to be crushed in the collision with these more substantial elements.

§ 17. In the narrowest, but most usual application of the term, we understand by "education" the influence of the individual upon the individual, exerted with the object of developing his powers in a conscious and methodical manner, either generally or in special directions, the educator being relatively mature, and exercising authority over the relatively immature pupil. Without authority on the one hand and obedience on the other, education would lack its ethical basis—a neglect of the will-training could not be compensated for by any amount of knowledge or smartness.

§ 18. The general province of education includes the development of the individual into the theoretical and practical reason immanent in him. The definition which limits education to the development of the individual into ethical customs (obedience to morality, social conventionalities, and the laws of the state—Hegel's definition is here referred to: "The object of education is to make men ethical") is not comprehensive enough, because it ignores the side of the *intellect*, and takes note only of the *will*. The individual should not only be man in general (as he is through the adoption of moral and ethical forms—which are *general* forms, customs, or laws, and thus the forms imposed by the *will* of the *race*), but he should also be a self-conscious subject, a particular individual (man, through his intellect, exists for himself as an individual, while through his general habits and customs he loses his individuality and spontaneity).

§ 19. Education has a definite object in view and it proceeds by grades of progress toward it. The systematic tendency is essential to all education, properly so called.

§ 20. Division of labor has become requisite in the higher spheres of teaching. The growing multiplicity of branches of knowledge creates the necessity for the specialist as teacher. With this tendency to specialties it becomes more and more difficult to preserve what is so essential to the pupil—his rounded human culture and symmetry of development. The citizen of modern civilization sometimes appears to be an artificial product by the side of the versatility of the savage man.

§ 21. From this necessity of the division of labor in modern times there arises the demand for two kinds of educational institutions—those devoted to general education (common schools, colleges, etc.), and special schools (for agriculture, medicine, mechanic arts, etc).

§ 22. The infinite possibility of culture for the individual leaves, of course, his actual accomplishment a mere approximation to a complete education. Born idiots are excluded from the possibility of education, because the lack of universal ideas in their consciousness precludes to that class of unfortunates anything beyond a mere mechanical training.

§ 23. Spirit, or mind, makes its own nature; it *is* what it produces—a self-result. From this follows the *form* of education. It commences with (1) undeveloped mind—that of the infant—wherein nearly all is potential, and but little is actualized; (2) its first stage of development is self-estrangement—it is absorbed in the observation of objects around it; (3) but it discovers laws and principles (universality) in external nature, and finally identifies them with reason—it comes to recognize itself in nature—to recognize conscious mind as the creator and preserver of the external world—and thus becomes at home in nature. Education does not create, but it emancipates.

§ 24. This process of self-estrangement and its removal belongs to all culture. The mind must fix its attention upon what is foreign to it, and penetrate its disguise. It will discover its own substance under the seeming alien being. Wonder is the accompaniment of this stage of estrangement. The love of travel and adventure arises from this basis.

§ 25. Labor is distinguished from play: The former concentrates its energies on some object, with the purpose of making it conform to its will and purpose; play occupies itself with its object according to its caprice and arbitrariness, and has no care for the results or products of its activity; work is prescribed by authority, while play is necessarily spontaneous.

§ 26. Work and Play: the distinction between them. In play the child feels that he has entire control over the object with which he is dealing, both in respect to its existence and the object for which it exists. His arbitrary will may change both with perfect impunity, since all depends upon his caprice; he exercises his powers in play according to his natural proclivities, and therein finds scope to develope his own individuality. In work, on the contrary, he must have respect for the object with which he deals. It must be held sacred against his caprice, must not be destroyed nor injured in any way, and its object must likewise be respected. His own personal inclinations must be entirely subordinated, and the business that he is at work upon must be carried forward in accordance with its own ends and aims, and without reference to his own feelings in the matter.

Thus work teaches the pupil the lesson of self-sacrifice (the right of superiority which the general interest possesses over the particular), while play develops his personal idiosyncrasy.

§ 27. Without play, the child would become more and more a machine, and lose all freshness and spontaneity—all originality. Without work, he would develop into a monster of caprice and arbitrariness.

From the fact that man must learn to combine with man, in order that the individual may avail himself of the experience and labors of his fellow-men, self-sacrifice for the sake of combination is the great lesson of life. But as this should be *voluntary* self-sacrifice, education must train the child equally in the two directions of spontaneity and obedience. The educated man finds recreation in change of work.

§ 28. Education seeks to assimilate its object—to make what was alien and strange to the pupil into something familiar and habitual to him. [The pupil is to attack, one after the other, the foreign realms in the world of nature and man, and conquer them for his own, so that he can be "at home" in them. It is the necessary condition of all growth, all culture, that one widens his own individuality by this conquest of new provinces alien to him. By this the individual transcends the narrow limits of particularity and becomes generic—the individual becomes the species. A good definition of education is this: it is the process by which the individual man elevates himself to the species.]

§ 29. (1) Therefore, the first requirement in education is that the pupil shall acquire the habit of subordinating his likes and dislikes to the attainment of a rational object.

It is necessary that he shall acquire this indifference to his own pleasure, even by employing his powers on that which does not appeal to his interest in the remotest degree.

§ 30. Habit soon makes us familiar with those subjects which seemed so remote from our personal interest, and they become agreeable to us. The objects, too, assume a new interest upon nearer approach, as being useful or injurious to us. That is useful which serves us as a means for the realization of a rational purpose; injurious, if it hinders such realization. It happens that objects are useful in one sense and injurious in another, and *vice versa.* Education must make the pupil capable of deciding on the usefulness of an object, by reference to its effect on his permanent vocation in life.

§ 31. But *good and evil* are the ethical distinctions which furnish the absolute standard to which to refer the question of the usefulness of objects and actions.

§ 32. (2) Habit is (a) *passive*, or (b) *active*. The passive habit is that which gives us the power to retain our equipoise of mind in the midst of a world of changes (pleasure and pain, grief and joy, etc). The active habit gives us skill, presence of mind, tact in emergencies, etc.

§ 33. (3) Education deals altogether with the formation of habits. For it aims to make some condition or form of activity into a second nature for the pupil. But this involves, also, the breaking up of previous habits. This power to break up habits, as well as to form them, is necessary to the freedom of the individual.

§ 34. Education deals with these complementary relations (antitheses): (a) authority and obedience; (b) rationality (*general* forms) and individuality; (c) work and play; (d) habit (general custom) and spontaneity. The development and reconciliation of these opposite sides in the pupil's character, so that they become his second nature, removes the phase of constraint which at first accompanies the formal inculcation of rules, and the performance of prescribed tasks. The freedom of the pupil is the ultimate object to be kept in view, but a too early use of freedom may work injury to the pupil. To remove a pupil from all temptation would be to remove possibilities of growth in strength to resist it; on the other hand, to expose him needlessly to temptation is fiendish.

§ 35. Deformities of character in the pupil should be carefully traced back to their origin, so that they may be explained by their history. Only by comprehending the historic growth of an organic defect are we able to prescribe the best remedies.

§ 36. If the negative behavior of the pupil (his bad behavior) results from ignorance due to his own neglect, or to his wilfulness, it should be met directly by an act of authority on the part of the teacher (and without an appeal to reason). An appeal should be made to the understanding of the pupil only when he is somewhat mature, or shows by his repetition of the offence that his proclivity is deep-seated, and requires an array of all good influences to reinforce his feeble resolutions to amend.

§ 37. Reproof, accompanied by threats of punishment, is apt to degenerate into scolding.

§ 38. After the failure of other means, punishment should be resorted to. Inasmuch as the punishment should be for the purpose of making the pupil realize that it is the consequence of his deed returning on himself, it should always be administered for some particular act of his, and this should be specified. The "overt act" is the only thing which a man can be held accountable for in a court of justice; although it is true that the harboring of evil thoughts or intentions is a sin, yet it is not a crime until realized in an overt act.

§ 40. Punishment should be regulated, not by abstract rules, but in view of the particular case and its attending circumstances.

§ 41. Sex and age of pupil should be regarded in prescribing the mode and degree of punishment. Corporal punishment is best for pupils who are very immature in mind; when they are more developed they may be punished by any imposed restraint upon their free wills which will isolate them from the ordinary routine followed by their fellow-pupils. (Deprivation of the right to do as others do is a wholesome species of punishment for those old or mature enough to feel its effects, for it tends to secure respect for the regular tasks by elevating them to the rank of rights and privileges.) For young men and women, the punishment should be of a kind that is based on a sense of honor.

§ 42. (1) Corporal punishment should be properly administered by means of the rod, subduing wilful defiance by the application of force.

§ 43. (2) Isolation makes the pupil realize a sense of his dependence upon human society, and upon the expression of this dependence by coöperation in the common tasks. Pupils should not be shut up in a dark room, nor removed from the personal supervision of the teacher. (To shut up two or more in a room without supervision is not isolation, but association; only it is association for mischief, and not for study.)

§ 44. (3) Punishment based on the sense of honor may or may not be based on isolation. It implies a state of maturity on the part of the pupil. Through his offence the pupil has destroyed his equality with his fellows, and has in reality, in his inmost nature, isolated himself from them. Corporal punishment is external, but it may be accompanied with a keen sense of dishonor. Isolation, also, may, to a pupil, who is sensitive to honor, be a severe blow to self-respect. But a punishment founded entirely on the sense of honor would be wholly internal, and have no external discomfort attached to it.

§ 45. The necessity of carefully adapting the punishment to the age and maturity of the pupil, renders it the most difficult part of the teacher's duties. It is essential that the air and manner of the teacher who punishes should be that of one who acts from a sense of painful duty, and not from any delight in being the cause of suffering. Not personal likes and dislikes, but the rational necessity which is over teacher and pupil alike, causes the infliction of pain on the pupil.

§ 46. Punishment is the final topic to be considered under the head of "Form of Education."

In the act of punishment the teacher abandons the legitimate province of education, which seeks to make the pupil rational or obedient to what is reasonable, as a habit, and from his own free will. The pupil is punished in order that he may be *made* to conform to the rational, by the application of constraint. Another will is substituted for the pupil's, and good behavior is produced, but not by the pupil's free act. While education finds a negative limit in punishment, it finds a positive limit in the accomplishment of its legitimate object, which is the emancipation of the pupil from the state of imbecility, as regards mental and moral self-control, into the ability to direct himself rationally. When the pupil has acquired the discipline which enables him to direct his studies properly, and to control his inclinations in such a manner as to pursue his work regularly, the teacher is no longer needed for him—he becomes his own teacher.

There may be two extreme views on this subject—the one tending towards the negative extreme of requiring the teacher to do everything for the pupil, substituting his will for that of the pupil, and the other view tending to the positive extreme, and leaving everything to the pupil, even before his will is trained into habits of self-control, or his mind provided with the necessary elementary branches requisite for the prosecution of further study.

§ 47. (1) The subjective limit of education (on the negative side) is to be found in the individuality of the pupil—the limit to his natural capacity.

§ 48. (2) The objective limit to education lies in the amount of time that the person may devote to his training. It, therefore, depends largely upon wealth, or other fortunate circumstances.

§ 49. (3) The absolute limit of education is the positive limit (see § 46), beyond which the youth passes into freedom from the school, as a necessary instrumentality for further culture.

§ 50. The pre-arranged pattern-making work of the school is now done, but self-education may and should go on indefinitely, and will go on if the education of the school has really arrived at its "absolute" limit—*i.e.*, has fitted the pupil for self-education. Emancipation from the school does not emancipate one from learning through his fellow-men. Man's spiritual life is one depending upon coöperation with his fellow-men. Each must avail himself of the experience of his fellow-men, and in turn communicate his own experience to the common fund of the race. Thus each lives the life of the whole, and all live for each. School-education gives the pupil the instrumentalities with which to enable him to participate in this fund of experience—this common life of the race. After school-education comes the still more valuable education, which, however, without the school, would be in a great measure impossible.

* * * * *

ERRATA.

§ 26. Last two paragraphs should be within quotation marks, being from an English author.

§ 29. The second and third paragraphs belong to § 30.—the numbering being omitted.

§ 33. Line three—"instructive" should be "intuitive."

SECOND PART.

THE SPECIAL ELEMENTS OF EDUCATION.

§ 51. Education is the development of the theoretical and practical Reason which is inborn in the human being. Its end is to be accomplished by the labor which transforms a condition, existent at first only as an ideal, into a fixed habit, and changes the natural individuality into a glorified humanity. When the youth stands, so to speak, on his own feet, he is emancipated from education, and education then finds its limit. The special elements which may be said to make up education are the life, the cognition, and the will of man. Without the first, the real nature of the soul can never be made really to appear; without cognition, he can have no genuine will—*i.e.*, one of which he is conscious; and without will, no self-assurance, either of life or of cognition. It must not be forgotten that these three so-called elements are not to be held apart in the active work of education; for they are inseparable and continually interwoven the one with the other. But none the less do they determine their respective consequences, and sometimes one, sometimes another has the supremacy. In infancy, up to the fifth or sixth year, the physical development, or mere living, is the main consideration; the next period, that of childhood, is the time of acquiring knowledge, in which the child takes possession of the theory of the world as it is handed down—a tradition of the past, such as man has made it through his experience and insight; and finally, the period of youth must pave the way to a practical activity, the character of which the self-determination of the will must decide.

§ 52. We may, then, divide the elements of Pedagogics into three sections: (1) the physical, (2) the intellectual, (3) the practical. (The words "orthobiotics," "didactics," and "pragmatics" might be used to characterize them.)

Æsthetic training is only an element of the intellectual, as social, moral, and religious training are elements of the practical. But because these latter elements relate to external things (affairs of the world), the name pragmatics, is appropriate. In so far as education touches on the principles which underlie ethics, politics, and religion, it concurs with those sciences, but it is distinguished from them in the capacity which it imparts for solving the problems presented by the others.

The scientific order of topics must be established through the fact that the earlier, as the more abstract, constitute the condition of their presupposed end and aim, and the later because the more concrete constitute the ground of the former, and consequently their final cause, or the end for which they exist; just as in human beings, life in the order of time comes before cognition, and cognition before will, although life really presupposes cognition, and cognition will.

First Division.

Physical Education, or Orthobiotics.

§ 53. Only when we rightly comprehend the process of life may we know how to live aright. Life, the "circle of eternal change," is constantly transforming the inorganic into the organic, and after using it, returning it again to the realm of the inorganic. Whatever it does not assimilate of that which it has taken in simply as a stimulant, and whatever has become dead, it separates from itself and rejects. The organism is in perfect health when it accomplishes this double task of organizing and disorganizing. On the comprehension of this single fact all laws of physical health or of hygiene are based. This idea of the essence of life is expressed by Goethe in his Faust, where he sees the golden buckets perpetually rising and sinking.[13] When the equilibrium of the upward and downward motion is disturbed, we have disease. When the motion ceases we have death, in which the whole organism becomes inorganic, and the "dust returns to dust."

---

[13] Faust; Part I., Scene I. "How all weaves itself into the Whole! Each works and lives in the other! How the heavenly influences ascend and descend, and reach each other the golden buckets!"

§ 54. It follows from this that not only in the organism as a whole, but in every organ, and every part of every organ, this restless change of the inorganic to the organic is going on. Every cell has its own history, and this history is only the same as that of the whole of which it forms a part. Activity is then not inimical to the organism, but is the appointed means by which the progressive and retrogressive metamorphoses must be carried out. In order that the process may go on harmoniously, or, in other words, that the body may be healthy, the whole organism, and every part of it in its own way, must have its period of productive activity and then also its period of rest in which it finds renewal of strength for another period of activity. Thus we have waking and sleep, inspiration and expiration of air. Periodicity is the law of life. When we understand the relative antagonism (their stage of tension) of the different organs, and their cycles of activity, we shall hold the secret of the constant self-renewal of life. This thought finds expression in the old fairy stories of "The Search after the Fountain of Youth." And the figure of the fountain, with its rising and falling waters, doubtless finds its origin in the dim comprehension of the endless double movement, or periodicity of life.

§ 55. When to any organ, or to the whole organism, not sufficient time is allowed for it to withdraw into itself and to repair waste, we are conscious of fatigue. While the other organs all rest, however, one special organ may, as if separated from them, sustain a long-continued effort of activity even to the point of fatigue, without injury—as, *e.g.*, the lungs in talking while all the other members are at rest. But, on the other hand, it is not well to talk and run at the same time. The idea that the body may be preserved in a healthy state longer by sparing it—*i.e.*, by inactivity—is an error which springs from a false and mechanical conception of life. It is just as foolish to imagine that health depends on the abundance and excellence of food, for without the power of assimilating the food taken, nourishment of whatever kind does more harm than good; all real strength develops from activity alone.

§ 56. Physical education, according as it relates to the repairing, the muscular, or the emotional activities, is divided into (1) dietetics, (2) gymnastics, (3) sexual education. In the direct activity of life these all interact with each other, but for our purposes we are obliged to speak of them as if they worked independently. Moreover, in the development of the human being, they come into maturity of development in a certain order:

nutrition, muscular growth, sexual maturity. But Pedagogics can treat of these only as they are found in the infant, the child, and the youth; for with the arrival of mature life, education is over.

First Chapter.

Dietetics.

§ 57. By dietetics we mean the art of repairing the constant waste of the system, and, in childhood, of also building it up to its full form and size. Since in reality each organism has its own way of doing this, the diatetical practice must vary somewhat with sex, age, temperament, occupation, and circumstances. The science of Pedagogics has then, in this department, only to enunciate general principles. If we go into details, we fall into triviality. Nothing can be of more importance for the whole life than the way in which the physical education is managed in the very first stages of development. So generally is this fact accepted, that almost every nation has its own distinct system, which has been carefully elaborated. Many of these systems, no doubt, are characterized by gross errors, and widely differ as to time, place, and character, and yet they all have a justification for their peculiar form.

§ 58. The best food for the infant in the first months of its life is its mother's milk. The employment of another nurse, if a general custom, as in France, is highly objectionable, since with the milk the child is likely to imbibe to some extent his physical and ethical nature. The milk of an animal can never supply the place to a child of that of its own mother. In Walter Scott's story of *The Fair Maid of Perth*, Eachim is represented as timorous by nature, having been nourished by a white doe after the death of his mother.

§ 59. When the teeth make their appearance, it is a sign that the child is ready for solid food; and yet, till the second teeth appear, light, half-solid food and vegetables should constitute the principal part of the diet.

§ 60. When the second teeth have come, then the organism demands both vegetable and animal food. Too much meat is, doubtless, harmful. But it is an error to suppose that man was intended to eat vegetables alone, and that, as some have said, the adoption of animal food is a sign of his degeneracy.

The Hindoos, who live principally on a vegetable diet, are not at all, as has been asserted, a mild and gentle race. A glance into their stories, especially their erotic poetry, proves them to be quite as passionate as any other people.

§ 61. Man is an omnivorous being. Children have, therefore, a natural desire to taste of every thing. With them, eating and drinking have still a poetic side, and there is a pleasure in them which is not wholly the mere pleasure of taste. Their proclivity to taste of every thing should not, therefore, be harshly censured, unless it is associated with disobedience, or pursued in a clandestine manner, or when it betrays cunning and greediness.

§ 62. Children need much sleep, because they are growing and changing so fast. In later years, waking and sleeping must be regulated, and yet not too exactly.

§ 63. The clothing of children should follow the form of the body, and should be large enough to give them free room for the unfettered movement of every limb in play.

The Germans do more rationally for children in the matter of sleep and of dress than in that of food, which they often make too rich, and accompany with coffee, tea, etc. The clothing should be not only suitable in shape and size, it must also be made of simple and inexpensive material, so that the child may not be hampered in his play by the constant anxiety that a spot or a rent may cause fault to be found with him. If we foster in the child's mind too much thought about his clothes, we tend to produce either a narrow-mindedness, which treats affairs of the moment with too much respect and concerns itself with little things, or an empty vanity. Vanity is often produced by dressing children in a manner that attracts attention. (No one can fail to remark the peculiar healthful gayety of German children, and to contrast it with the different appearance of American children. It is undoubtedly true that the climate has much to do with this result, but it is also true that we may learn much from that nation in our way of treating children. Already we import their children's story-books, to the infinite delight of the little ones, and copies of their children's pictures are appropriated constantly by our children's magazines and picture-books. It is to be greatly desired that we should adopt the very sensible custom which prevails in Germany, of giving to each child its own little bed to sleep in, no matter how many may be required; and, in general, we shall not go far astray if we follow the

Germans in their treatment of their happy children.)

§ 64. Cleanliness is a virtue to which children should be trained, not only for the sake of their physical health, but also because it has a decided moral influence. Cleanliness will not have things deprived of their distinctive and individual character, and become again a part of original chaos. It is only a form of order which remands all things, dirt included, to their own places, and will not endure to have things mixed and confused. All adaptation in dress comes from this same principle. When every thing is in its proper place, all dressing will be suitable to the occasion and to the wearer, and the era of good taste in dress will have come. Dirt itself, as Lord Palmerston so wittily said, is nothing but "matter out of place." Cleanliness would hold every individual thing strictly to its differences from other things, and for the reason that it makes pure air, cleanliness of his own body, of his clothing, and of all his surroundings really necessary to man, it develops in him the feeling for the proper limitations of all existent things. (Emerson says: "Therefore is space and therefore is time, that men may know that things are not huddled and lumped, but sundered and divisible." He might have said, "Therefore is cleanliness.")

Second Chapter.

Gymnastics.

§ 65. Gymnastics is the art of cultivating in a rational manner the muscular system. The activity of the voluntary muscles, which are under the control of the brain, in distinction from the involuntary, which are under the control of the spinal cord, renders possible the connection of man with the external world, and acts in a reflex manner back upon the involuntary or automatic muscles for the purposes of repair and sensation. Because the activity of muscle-fibre consists in the change from contraction to expansion, and the reverse, gymnastics must use a constant change of movements which shall not only make tense, but relax the muscles that are to be exercised.

§ 66. The gymnastic art among any people will always bear a certain relation to its art of war. So long as fighting consists mainly of personal, hand-to-hand encounters of two combatants, so long will gymnastics turn its chief effort towards the development of the greatest possible amount of individual strength and dexterity. But after the invention of fire-arms of long range has changed the whole idea of war, the individual becomes only one member of a body, the army, the division, or the regiment, and emerges from this position into his individuality again only occasionally, as in sharpshooting, in the onset, or in the retreat. Modern gymnastics, as an art, can never be the same as the ancient art, for this very reason: that because of the loss of the individual man in the general mass of combatants, the matter of personal bravery is not of so much importance as formerly. The same essential difference between ancient and modern gymnastics, would result from the subjective, or internal character of the modern spirit. It is impossible for us, in modern times, to devote so much thought to the care of the body and to the reverential admiration of its beauty as did the Greeks.

The Turners' Unions and Turners' Halls in Germany belonged to the period of intense political enthusiasm in the German youth, and had a political significance. Now they have come back again to their place as an instrument of education, and seem in great cities to be of much importance. In mountainous countries, and in country life generally, a definite gymnastic drill is of much less importance, for much and varied exercise is of necessity a constant part of the daily life of every one.

The constant opportunity and the impulse to recreation helps in the same direction. In cities, on the contrary, there is not free space enough either in houses or yards for children to romp to their heart's and body's content. For this reason a gymnasium is here useful, so that they may have companionship in their plays. For girls this exercise is less necessary. Dancing may take its place, and systematic exercise should be used only where there is a tendency to some weakness or deformity. They are not to become Amazons. On the other hand, boys need the feeling of comradeship. It is true they find this in some measure in school, but they are not there perfectly on an equality, because the standing is determined to some extent by his intellectual ability. The academic youth cannot hope to win any great preëminence in the gymnastic hall, and running, climbing, leaping, and lifting do not interest him very much as he grows older. He takes a far more lively interest in exercises which have a military character. In Germany the gymnastic art is very closely united with the art of war.

(The German idea of a woman's whole duty—to knit, to sew, and to obey implicitly—is perhaps accountable for what Rosenkranz here says of exercise as regards girls. We, however, who know that the most frequent direct cause of debility and suffering in our young women is simply and solely a want of muscular strength, may be pardoned for dissenting from his opinion, and for suggesting that dancing is not a sufficient equivalent for the more violent games of their brothers. We do not fear to render them Amazons by giving them more genuine and systematic exercise, both physically and intellectually.)

§ 67. The main idea of gymnastics, and indeed of all exercise, is to give the mind control over its natural impulses, to make it master of the body which it inhabits, and of itself. Strength and dexterity must combine to give us a sense of mastership. Strength by itself produces the athlete, dexterity by itself the acrobat. Pedagogics must avoid both these extremes. Neither must it base its teaching of gymnastics on the idea of utility—as, *e.g.*, that man might save his life by swimming, should he fall into the water, and hence swimming should be taught, etc.

The main thought must be always to enable the soul to take full and perfect possession of the organism, so as not to have the body form a limit or fetter to its action in its dealings with the external world. We are to give it a perfect instrument in the body, in so far as our care may do so. Then we are to teach it to use that instrument, and exercise it in that use till it is complete master thereof.

(What is said about the impropriety of making athletes and acrobats may with justice be also applied to what is called "vocal gymnastics;" whence it comes that we have too often vocal athletes and acrobats in our graduates, and few readers who can read at sight, without difficulty or hesitation, and with appreciation or enjoyment, one page of good English.)

§ 68. There are all grades of gymnastic exercises, from the simple to the most complex, constituting a system. At first sight, there seems to be so much arbitrariness in these things that it is always very satisfactory to the mind to detect some rational system in them. Thus we have movements (*a*) of the lower extremities, (*b*) of the upper, (*c*) of the whole body, with corresponding movements, alternately, of the upper and of the lower extremities. We thus have leg, arm, and trunk movements.

§ 69. (1) The first set of movements, those of the legs and feet, are of prime importance, because upon them depends the carriage of the whole body. They are (*a*) walking, (*b*) running, (*c*) leaping; and each of these, also, may have varieties. We may have high and low leaping, and running may be distinguished as to whether it is to be a short and rapid, or a slow and long-continued movement. We may also walk on stilts, or run on skates. We may leap with a pole, or without one. Dancing is only an artistic and graceful combination of these movements.

§ 70. (2) The second set comprises the arm movements, which are about the same as the preceding, being (*a*) lifting, (*b*) swinging; (*c*) throwing. The use of horizontal poles and bars, as well as climbing and dragging, belong to lifting. Under throwing, come quoit and ball-playing and bowling. These movements are distinguished from each other not only quantitatively, but qualitatively; as, for instance, running is not merely rapid walking; it is a different kind of movement from walking, as the position of the extended and contracted muscles is different.

§ 71. (3) The third set of exercises, those of the trunk, differ from the other two, which should precede it, in that they bring the body into contact with an object in itself capable of active resistance, which it has to subdue. This object may be an element (water), an animal, or a human being; and thus we have (*a*) swimming, (*b*) riding, (*c*) fighting in single combat. In swimming we have the elastic fluid, water, to overcome by means of arm and leg movements. This may be made very difficult by a strong current, or by rough water, and yet we always have here to strive against an inanimate object. On the contrary, in horseback riding we have to deal with something that has a self of its own, and the contest challenges not our strength alone, but also our skill and courage. The motion is therefore very complex, and the rider must be able to exercise either or all of these qualities at need. But his attention must not be wholly given to his horse, for he has to observe also the road, and indeed every thing around him. One of the greatest advantages of horseback riding to the overworked student or the business man lies doubtlessly in the mental effort. It is impossible for him to go on revolving in his mind the problems or the thoughts which have so wearied or perplexed him. His whole attention is incessantly demanded for the management of his horse, for the observation of the road, which changes its character with every step, and with the objects, far or near, which are likely to attract the attention of the animal he rides. Much good, doubtless, results from the exercise of the muscles of the trunk, which are not in any other motion called into such active play, but much also from the unavoidable distraction of the mind from the ordinary routine of thought, which is the thing most needed. When the object which we are to subdue, instead of being an animal, is a man like ourselves, as in single combat, we have exercise both of body and mind pushed to its highest power. We have then to oppose an intelligence which is equal to our own, and no longer the intelligence of an unreasoning animal. Single combat is the truly chivalrous exercise; and this also, as in the old chivalry time, may be combined with horsemanship.

In single combat we find also a qualitative distinction, and this of three kinds: (*a*) boxing and wrestling, (*b*) fighting with canes or clubs, and (*c*) rapier and sword fencing. The Greeks carried wrestling to its highest pitch of excellence. Among the British, a nation of sailors, boxing is still retained as a national custom. Fencing with a cane or stick is much in use among the French artisan class. The cane is a sort of refined club. When the sword or rapier makes its appearance, we come to mortal combat. The southern European excels in the use of the rapier; the Germans in that of the sword. The appearance of the pistol marks the degeneracy of the art of single combat, as it makes the weak man equal to the strong, and there is therefore no more incentive to train the body to strength in order to overcome an enemy. (The trained intelligence, the quick eye, the steady hand, the wary thought to perceive and to take advantage of an opportunity—these are the qualities which the invention of gunpowder set up above strength and brute force. The Greek nation, and we may say Greek mythology and art, would have been impossible with gunpowder; the American nation impossible without it.)

Third Chapter.

Sexual Education.

[This chapter is designed for parents rather than for teachers, and is hence not paraphrased here. A few observations are, however, in place.] Great care is necessary at the period of youth that a rational system of food and exercise be maintained. But the general fault is in the omission of this care in preceding years. One cannot neglect due precautions for many years, and then hope to repair the damage caused, by extreme care for one or two years.

Special care is necessary that the brain be not overworked in early years, and a morbid excitation of the whole nervous system thereby induced. We desire to repress any tendency to the rapid development of the nervous system. Above all, is the reading of the child to be carefully watched and guarded. Nothing can be worse food for a child than what are called sensational romances. That the reading of such tends to enfeeble and enervate the whole thinking power is a fact which properly belongs to the intellectual side of our question not yet reached, and may be here merely mentioned. But the effect on the physical condition of the youth, of such carelessly written sensational stories, mostly of the French type, and full of sensuous, if not sensual suggestions, is a point not often enough considered. The teacher cannot, perhaps, except indirectly, prevent the reading of such trash at home. But every influence which he can bring to bear towards the formation of a purer and more correct taste, he should never omit. Where there is a public library in the town, he should make himself acquainted with its contents, and give the children direct help in their selection of books.

This is an external means. But he should never forget that every influence which he can bring to bear in his daily work to make science pleasant and attractive, and every lesson which he gives in the use of pure, correct English, free from exaggeration, from slang, and from mannerism, goes far to render such miserable and pernicious trash distasteful even to the child himself.

Every example of thorough work, every pleasure that comes from the solving of a problem or the acquisition of a new fact, is so much fortification against the advances of the enemy; while all shallow half work, all pretence or show tend to create an appetite in the child's mind which shall demand such food.

The true teacher should always have in his mind these far-away and subtle effects of his teaching; not present good or pleasure either for himself or his pupil, but the far-off good—the distant development. That idea would free him from the notion, too common in our day, that the success or failure of his efforts is to be tested by any adroitly contrived system of examinations; or still worse, exhibitions. His success can alone be tested by the future lives of his pupils—by their love for, or dislike of, new knowledge. His success will be marked by their active growth through all their lives; his failure, by their early arrested development.

AN OUTLINE OF EDUCATIONAL PSYCHOLOGY.

BY WM. T. HARRIS.

[TO BE USED AS AN INTRODUCTION TO PARAGRAPHS 81 TO 102 OF ROSENKRANZ'S PEDAGOGICS.]

I.

> What beings can be educated; the plant has reaction against its surroundings in the form of nutrition; the animal has reaction in the form of nutrition and feeling; Aristotle calls the life of the plant the "nutritive soul," and the life of the animal the "sensitive soul."
>
> The life of the plant is a continual reproduction of new individuals—a process of going out of one individual into another—so that the particular individual loses its identity, although the identity of the species is preserved.

That which is dependent upon external circumstances, and is only a circumstance itself, is not capable of education. Only a "self" can be educated; and a "self" is a conscious unity—a "self-activity," a being which is through itself, and not one that is made by surrounding conditions.

Again, in order that a being possess a capacity for education, it must have the ability to realize within itself what belongs to its species or race.

If an acorn could develop itself so that it could realize, not only its own possibility as an oak, but its entire species, and all the varieties of oaks within itself, and without losing its particular individuality, it would possess the capacity for education. But an acorn, in reality, cannot develop its possibility without the destruction of its own individuality. The acorn vanishes in the oak tree, and the crop of acorns which succeeds is not again the same acorn, except in *kind* or species. "The species lives, but the individual dies," in the vegetable world.

So it is in the animal world. The brute lives his particular life, unable to develop within himself the form of his entire species, and still less the form of all animal life. And yet the animal possesses self-activity in the powers of locomotion, sense-perception, feeling, emotion, and other elementary shapes. Both animal and plant react against surroundings, and possess more or less power to assimilate what is foreign to them. The plant takes moisture and elementary inorganic substances, and converts them into nutrition wherewith to build its cellular growth. The animal has not only this power of nutrition, which assimilates its surroundings, but also the power of *feeling*, which is a wonderful faculty. *Feeling* reproduces within the organism of the animal the external condition; it is an ideal reproduction of the surroundings. The environment of the plant may be seized upon and appropriated in the form of sap, or in the form of carbonic acid, for the nourishment of that plant; but there is no ideal reproduction of the environment in the form of *feeling*, as in the animal.

In the activity of *feeling*, the animal transcends his material, corporeal limits—lives beyond his mere body, and participates in the existence of all nature. He reproduces within himself the external. Such being the nature of the activity of *feeling*, which forms the distinguishing attribute that divides animals from plants, the question meets us at the outset, "Why is not the animal capable of education? Why can he not realize within himself his entire species or race, as man can?"

In order to settle this fundamental question, we must study carefully the scope and limits of this activity, which we have termed "Feeling," and which is known under many names—as, sensation, sensibility, sensitivity, sense-perception, intuition, and others.

Education aims to develop the mind as intellect and will. It must know what it is to develop, and learn to distinguish higher or more complete stages of intellect and will from those which are rudimentary.

Again, the discussion of mind begins properly with the first or most undeveloped manifestation—at the stage where it is common to brutes and human beings. Hence we may begin our study of educational psychology at this point where the distinction between animal and plant appears, and where the question of the capacity for education arises.

When we understand the relation of feeling or sensibility to the higher manifestations of mind, we shall see in what consists a capacity for education, and we shall learn many essentials in regard to the matter and method, the *what* and the *how* of education.

A general survey of the world discovers that there is inter-action among its parts. This is the verdict of science, as the systematic form of human experience. In the form of gravitation we understand that each body depends upon every other body, and the annihilation of a particle of matter in a body would cause a change in that body which would affect every other body in the physical universe. Even gravitation, therefore, is a manifestation of the whole universe in each part of it, although it is not a manifestation which exists *for* that part, because the part does not *know* it.

There are other forms wherein the whole manifests itself in each part of it—as, for example, in the phenomena of light, heat, and possibly in magnetism and electricity. These forms of manifestation of the external world upon an individual object are destructive to the individuality of the object. If the nature of a thing is stamped upon it from without, it is an element only, and not a self; it is dependent, and belongs to that on which it depends. It does not possess itself, but belongs to that which *makes* it, and which gives evidence of ownership by continually modifying it.

But the plant, as we just now said, has some degree of self-activity, and is not altogether made by the totality of external conditions. The growth of the plant is through assimilation of external substances. It reacts against its surroundings and digests them, and grows through the nutrition thus formed.

All beings that cannot react against surroundings and modify them, lack individuality. Individuality begins with this power of reaction and modification of external surroundings. Even the power of cohesion is a rudimentary form of reaction and of special individuality.

In the case of the plant, the reaction is *real*, but not also *ideal*. The plant acts upon its food, and digests it, or assimilates it, and imposes its *form* on that which it draws within its organism. It does not, however, reproduce within itself the externality as that external exists for itself. It does not form within itself an idea, or even a feeling of that which is external to it. Its participation in the external world is only that of *real* modification of it or through it; either the plant digests the external, or the external limits *it*, and prevents its growth, so that where one begins the other ceases. Hence it is that the elements—the matter of which the plant is composed, that which it has assimilated even—still retain a large degree of foreign power or force—a large degree of externality which the plant has not been able to annul or to digest. The plant-activity subdues its food, changes its shape and its place, subordinates it to its use; but what the matter brings with it, and still retains of the world beyond the plant, does not exist for the plant; the plant cannot read or interpret the rest of the universe from that small portion of it which it has taken up within its own organism. And yet the history of the universe is impressed on each particle of matter, as well within the plant as outside of it, and it could be understood were there capacities for recognizing it.

The reaction of the life of the plant upon the external world is not sufficient to constitute a fixed, abiding individuality. With each accretion there is some change of particular individuality. Every growth to a plant is by the sprouting out of new individuals—new plants—a ceaseless multiplication of individuals, and not the preservation of the same individual. The species is preserved, but not the particular individual. Each limb, each twig, even each leaf is a new individual, which grows out from the previous growth as the first sprout grew from the seed. Each part furnishes a soil for the next. When a plant no longer sends out new individuals, we say it is dead. The life of the plant is only a life of nutrition.

Aristotle called vegetable life "the nutritive soul," and the life of the animal the "feeling," or *sensitive* soul. Nutrition is only an activity of preservation of the general form in new individuals, it is only the life of the species, and not the life of the permanent individual.

Therefore we see that in the vegetable world we do not possess a being that can be educated—for no individual of it can realize *within* itself the species; its realization of the species is a continual process of going out of itself in new individuals, but no activity of *return* to itself, so as to preserve *the identity* of an individual.

II.

> Feeling is a unity of the parts of an organism everywhere present in it; feeling is also an ideal reproduction of the external surroundings; feeling is therefore a synthesis of the internal and external. Aristotle joins locomotion and desire to feeling, as correlates; how desire is a more explicit recognition of the unity of the external and internal than the first form of feeling is; feeling reproduces the external without destroying its externality, while nutrition receives the external only after it has destroyed its individuality and assimilated it; desire is the side of feeling that unfolds into will.

With feeling or sensibility we come to a being that reacts on the external world in a far higher manner, and realizes a more wonderful form of individuality.

The animal possesses, in common with the plant, a process of assimilation and nutrition. Moreover, he possesses a capacity to *feel*. Through *feeling*, or sensation, all of the parts of his extended organism are united in one centre. He is one individual, and not a bundle of separate individuals, as a plant is. With feeling, likewise, are joined *locomotion* and *desire*. For these are counterparts of feeling. He feels—*i.e.*, lives as one indivisible unity throughout his organism and controls it, and moves the parts of his body. Desire is more than mere feeling. Mere feeling alone is the perception of the external within the being, hence an ideal reproduction of the external world. In feeling, the animal exists not only within himself, but also passes over his limit, and has for object the reality of the external world that limits him. Hence it is the perception of his finiteness—his limits are his defects, his needs, wants, inadequateness—his separation from the world as a whole. In feeling, the animal perceives his separation from the rest of the world, and also his union with it. Feeling expands into desire when the external world, or some portion of it, is seen as ideally belonging to the limited unity of the animal being. It is beyond the limit, and ought to be assimilated within the limited individuality of the animal.

Mere *feeling*, when attentively considered, is found to contain these wonderful features of self-activity: it reproduces for itself the external world that limits it; it makes for itself an ideal object, which includes its own self and its not-self at the same time. It is a higher form than mere nutrition; for nutrition destroys the nature of such externality as it receives into itself, while feeling preserves the external in its foreign individuality.

But through *feeling* the animal ascends to *desire*, and sees the independent externality as an object for its acquisition, and through locomotion it is enabled to seize and appropriate it in a degree which the plant did not possess.

III.

> The various forms of feeling—its specialization: (*a*) touch, the feeling of mere limits, the indifferent external independence of the organism and its surroundings; (*b*) taste, the feeling of the external object when it is undergoing dissolution by assimilation; (*c*) smell, the feeling of chemical dissolution in general; (*d*) hearing, the feeling of the resistance of bodies against attacks: sound being vibration caused by elastic reaction against attacks on cohesion; (*e*) seeing, the feeling of objects in their independence, without dissolution or attack; plant life, nutrition, a process in which the individuality is not preserved either in time or in space; animal life, as feeling, preserves its individuality as regards space, but not as regards time.

Having noted these important characteristics of the lower orders of life, and found that *reaction* from the part against the whole—from the internal against the external—belongs to plant life and animal life, we may now briefly mention the ways in which feeling is particularized. In the lower animals it is only the feeling of touch; in higher organisms it becomes also localized as seeing, hearing, taste, and smell. These forms of sense-perception constitute a scale (as it were) of feeling. With touch, there is reproduction of externality, but the ideality of the reproduction is not so complete as in the other forms. With taste, the feeling cognizes the external object as undergoing dissolution, and assimilation within its own organism. We taste only what we are beginning to destroy by the first process of assimilation—that of eating. In smell, we perceive chemical dissolution of bodies. In seeing and hearing, we have the forms of *ideal* sensibility. Hearing perceives the attack made on the individuality of an external thing, and its reaction in vibrations, which reveal to us its internal nature—its cohesion, etc. In seeing, we have the highest form of sense-perception as the perception of things in their external independence—not as being destroyed chemically, like the objects of taste and smell; not as being attacked and resisting, like the objects which are known through the ear; not as mere limits to our organism, as in the sense of touch.

Sense-perception, as the developed realization of the activity of feeling, belongs to the animal creation, including man as an animal.

We have not yet, therefore, answered the question of capacity for education, so far as it concerns a discrimination between man and the brute. We have only arrived at the conclusion that the vegetable world does not possess the capacity for education, because its individual specimens are no complete individuals, but only transitory phases manifesting the species by continual reproduction of new individuals which are as incomplete as the old ones. Plant life does not possess that self-activity which returns into itself in the same individual—if we may so express it; it goes out of one individual into another perpetually. Its identity is that of the *species*, but not of the *individual*.

How is it with the animal—with the being which possesses sensibility, or feeling? This question recurs. In feeling there is a reaction, just as in the plant. This reaction is, however, in an ideal form—the reproduction of the external without assimilation of it—and especially is this the case in the sense of *sight*, though it is true of all forms of sensation to a less degree.

But all forms of sensibility are limited and special; they refer only to the *present*, in its forms of *here* and *now*. The animal cannot feel what is not here and now. Even seeing is limited to what is present before it. When we reflect upon the significance of this limitation of sense-perception, we shall find that we need some higher form of self-activity still before we can realize the species in the individual *i.e.*, before we can obtain the true individual—the permanent individuality.

The defect in plant life was, that there was neither identity of individuality in space nor identity in time. The growth of the plant destroyed the individuality of the seed with which we began, so that it was evanescent in time; it served only as the starting-point for new individualities, which likewise, in turn, served again the same purpose; and so its growth in space was a departure from itself as individual.

The animal is a preservation of individuality as regards space. He returns into himself in the form of *feeling* or *sensibility*; but as regards time, it is not so—feeling being limited to the present. Without a higher activity than feeling, there is no continuity of individuality in the animal any more than in the plant. Each new moment is a new beginning to a being that has feeling, but not memory.

Thus the individuality of mere feeling, although a far more perfect realization of individuality than that found in plant life, is yet, after all, not a continuous individuality for itself, but only for the species.

In spite of the ideal self-activity which appertains to feeling, even in sense-perception, only the species lives in the animal and the individual dies, unless there be higher forms of activity.

IV.

> Representation is the next form above sense-perception. The lowest phase of representation is recollection, which simply repeats for itself a former sense-perception or series of sense-perceptions; in representation the mind is free as regards external impressions; it does not require the presence of the object, but recalls it without its own time and place; fancy and imagination are next higher than recollection, because the mind not only recalls images, but makes new combinations of them, or creates them altogether; attention is the appearance of the will in the intellect; with attention begins the separation of the transient from the variable in perception; memory is the highest form of representation;

memory deals with general forms—not mere images of experience, but general types of objects of perception; memory, in this sense, is productive as well as reproductive; with memory arises language.

Here we pass over to the consideration of higher forms of intellect and will.

While mere sensation, as such, acts only in the presence of the object—reproducing (ideally), it is true, the external object, the faculty of representation is a higher form of self-activity (or of reaction against surrounding conditions), because it can recall, at its own pleasure, the ideal object. Here is the beginning of emancipation from the limitations of time.

The self-activity of representation can summon before it the object that is no longer present to it. Hence its activity is now a double one, for it can seize not only what is now and here immediately before it, but it can compare this present object with the past, and identify or distinguish between the two. Thus recollection or representation may become *memory*.

As memory, the mind achieves a form of activity far above that of sense-perception or mere recollection. It must be noted carefully that mere recollection or representation, although it holds fast the perception in time (making it permanent), does not necessarily constitute an activity completely emancipated from time, nor indeed very far advanced towards it. It is only the beginning of such emancipation. For mere recollection stands in the presence of the special object of sense-perception; although the object is no longer present to the senses (or to mere feeling), yet the image is present to the representative perception, and is just as much a particular here and now as the object of sense-perception. There intervenes a new activity on the part of the soul before it arrives at memory. Recollection is not memory, but it is the activity which grows into it by the aid of the activity of attention.

The special characteristics of objects of the senses are allowed to drop away, in so far as they are unessential and merely circumstantial, and gradually there arises in the mind the type—the *general form*—of the object perceived. This general form is the object of memory. Memory deals therefore with what is general, and a type, rather than with what is directly recollected or perceived.

The activity by which the mind ascends from sense-perception to memory is the activity of attention. Here we have the appearance of the will in intellectual activity. Attention is the control of perception by means of the will. The senses shall no longer passively receive and report what is before them, but they shall choose some definite point of observation, and neglect all the rest.

Here, in the act of attention we find *abstraction*, and the greater attainment of freedom by the mind. The mind abstracts its view from the many things before it, and concentrates on one point.

Educators have for many ages noted that the habit of attention is the first step in intellectual education. With it we have found the point of separation between the animal intellect and the human. Not attention simply—like that with which the cat watches by the hole of a mouse—but attention which arrives at results of abstraction, is the distinguishing characteristic of educative beings.

Attention abstracts from some things before it and concentrates on others. Through attention grows the capacity to discriminate between the special, particular object and its general type. Generalization arises, but not what is usually called generalization—only a more elementary form of it. Memory, as the highest form of representation—distinguishing it from mere recollection, which reproduces only what has been perceived—such memory deals with the general forms of objects, their continuity in time. Such activity of memory, therefore, does not reproduce mere images, but only the concepts or general ideas of things, and therefore it belongs to the stage of mind that uses language.

V.

> Language marks the arrival at the stage of thought—at the stage of the perception of universals—hence at the possibility of education; language fixes the general types which the productive memory forms; each one of these types, indicated by a word, stands for a possible infinite of sense-perceptions or recollections; the word *tree* stands for all the trees that exist, and for all that have existed or will

> exist. Animals do not create for themselves a new world of general types, but deal only with the first world of particular objects; hence they are lost in the variety and multiplicity of continuous succession and difference. Man's sense-perception is with memory; hence always a recognition of the object as not wholly new, but only as an example of what he is mostly familiar with. Intellectual education has for its object the cultivation of reflection; reflection is the Platonic "Reminiscence," which retraces the unconscious processes of thought.

Language is the means of distinguishing between the brute and the human—between the animal soul, which has continuity only in the species (which pervades its being in the form of *instinct*), and the *human*, soul, which is immortal, and possessed of a capacity to be educated.

There is no language until the mind can perceive general types of existence; mere proper names nor mere exclamations or cries do not constitute language. All words that belong to language are significative—they "*express*" or "*mean*" something—hence they are conventional symbols, and not mere individual designations. Language arises only through common consent, and is not an invention of one individual. It is a product of individuals acting together as a community, and hence implies the ascent of the individual into the species. Unless an individual could ascend into the species he could not *understand* language. To know words and their meaning is an activity of divine significance; it denotes the formation of universals in the mind—the ascent above the here and now of the senses, and above the representation of mere images, to the activity which grasps together the general conception of objects, and thus reaches beyond what is transient and variable.

Doubtless the nobler species of animals possess not only sense-perception, but a considerable degree of the power of representation. They are not only able to recollect, but to imagine or fancy to some extent, as is evidenced by their dreams. But that animals do not generalize sufficiently to form for themselves a new objective world of types and general concepts, we have a sufficient evidence in the fact that they do not use words, or invent conventional symbols. With the activity of the symbol-making form of representation, which we have named Memory, and whose evidence is the invention and use of language, the true form of individuality is attained, and each individual human being, as mind, may be said to be the entire species. Inasmuch as he can form universals in his mind, he can realize the most abstract thought; and he is conscious. Consciousness begins when one can seize the pure universal in the presence of immediate objects here and now.

The sense-perception of the mere animal, therefore, differs from that of the human being in this:—

The human being knows himself as subject that sees the object, while the animal sees the object, but does not separate himself, as universal, from the special act of seeing. To know that I am I, is to know the most general of objects, and to carry out abstraction to its very last degree; and yet this is what all human beings do, young or old, savage or civilized. The savage invents and uses language—an act of the species, but which the species cannot do without the participation of the individual.

It should be carefully noted that this activity of generalization which produces language, and characterizes the human from the brute, is not the generalization of the activity of thought, so-called.

It is the preparation for thought. These general types of things are the things which thought deals with. Thought does not deal with mere immediate objects of the senses; it deals rather with the objects which are indicated by words—*i.e.*, general objects.

Some writers would have us suppose that we do not arrive at general notions except by the process of classification and abstraction, in the mechanical manner that they lay down for this purpose. The fact is that the mind has arrived at these general ideas in the process of learning language. In infancy, most children have learned such words as *is*, *existence*, *being*, *nothing*, *motion*, *cause*, *change*, *I*, *you*, *he*, etc., etc.

But the point is not the mere arrival at these ideas. Education does not concern itself with that; it does not concern itself with children who have not yet learned to talk—that is left for the nursery.

It is the process of becoming conscious of these ideas by reflection, with which we have to concern ourselves in education. Reflection is everywhere the object of education. Even when the school undertakes to teach pupils the correct method of observation—how to use the senses, as in "object-lessons"—it all means *reflective* observation, *conscious* use of the senses; it would put this in the place of the *naïve* spontaneity which characterizes the first stages of sense-perception.

We must not underrate these precepts of pedagogy because we find that they are not what it claims for them—*i.e.*, they are not methods of first discovery, and of arrival at principles, but only methods of reflection, and of recognizing what we have already learned. We see that Plato's "Reminiscence" was a true form of statement for the perception of truths of reflection. The first knowing is utterly unconscious of its own method; the second or scientific form of knowing, which education develops, is a knowing in which the mind knows its method. Hence it is a knowing which knows its own necessity and universality.

VI.

> Education presupposes the stage of mind reached in productive memory; it deals with reflection; four stages of reflection: (*a*) sensuous ideas perceive things; (*b*) abstract ideas perceive forces or elements of a process; (*c*) concrete idea perceives one process, a pantheistic first principle, persistent force; (*d*) absolute idea perceives a conscious first principle, absolute person.

We have considered in our psychological study thus far the forms of life and cognition, contrasting the phase of nutrition with that of feeling, or sensibility. We have seen the various forms of feeling in sense-perception, and the various forms of representation as the second phase of intellectual activity—the forms of recollection, fancy, imagination, attention, and memory. We draw the line between the animals capable of education and those not capable of it, at the point of memory defined—not as recollection, but as the faculty of general ideas or conceptions, to which the significant words of language correspond.

With the arrival at language, we arrive at education in the human sense of the term; with the arrival at language, we arrive at the view of the world at which thought as a mental process begins. As sense-perception has before it a world of *present* objects, so thought has before it a world of general concepts, which language has defined and fixed.

It is true that few persons are aware that language stands for a world of general ideas, and that reflection has to do with this world of universals. Hence it is, too, that so much of the so-called science of education is very crude and impractical. Much of it is materialistic, and does not recognize the self-activity of mind; but makes it out to be a correlation of physical energies—derived from the transmutation of food by the process of digestion, and then by the brain converted into thought.

Let us consider now the psychology of thinking, or reflection, and at first in its most inadequate forms. As a human process, the knowing is always a knowing by universals—a re-cognition, and not simple apprehension, such as the animals, or such as beings have that do not use language. The process of development of stages of thought begins with sensuous ideas, which perceive mere individual, concrete, real objects, as it supposes. In conceiving these, it uses language and thinks general ideas, but it does not know it, nor is it conscious of the relations involved in such objects. This is the first stage of reflection. The world exists for it as an innumerable congeries of things, each one independent of the other, and possessing self-existence. It is the stand-point from which atomism would be adopted as the philosophic system. Ask it what the ultimate principle of existence is, and it would reply, "Atoms."

But this view of the world is a very unstable one, and requires very little reflection to overturn it, and bring one to the next basis—that of *abstract ideas*. When the mind looks carefully at the world of things, it finds that there is dependence and interdependence. Each object is related to something else, and changes when that changes. Each object is a part of a process that is going on. The process produced it, and the process will destroy it—nay, it is destroying it now, while we look at it. We find, therefore, that things are not the true beings which we thought them to be, but processes *are* the reality. Science takes this attitude, and studies out the history of each thing in its rise and its disappearance, and it calls this history the truth. This stage of thinking does not believe in *atoms* or in *things*; it believes in *forces* and *processes*—"abstract ideas"—because they are negative, and cannot be seen by the senses. This is the dynamic stand-point in philosophy.

Reflection knows that these abstract ideas possess more truth, more reality, than the "things" of sense-perception; the force is more real than the thing, because it outlasts a thing,—it causes things to originate, and to change, and disappear.

This stage of abstract ideas or of negative powers or forces finally becomes convinced of the essential unity of all processes and of all forces; it sets up the doctrine of the *correlation of forces*, and believes that persistent force is the ultimate truth, the fundamental reality of the world. This we may call a concrete idea, for it sets up a principle which is the origin of all things and forces, and also the destroyer of all things, and hence more real than the world of things and forces; and because this idea, when carefully thought out, proves to be the idea of self-determination—self-activity.

Persistent force, as taught us by the scientific men of our day, is the sole ultimate principle, and as such it gives rise to all existence by its self-activity, for there is nothing else for it to act upon. It causes all origins, all changes, and all evanescence. It gives rise to the particular forces—heat, light, electricity, magnetism, etc.—which in their turn cause the evanescent forms which sense-perception sees as "things."

We have described three phases:—

I. Sensuous Ideas perceive "things."
II. Abstract Ideas perceive "forces."
III. Concrete Idea perceives "persistent force."

In this progress from one phase of reflection to another, the intellect advances to a deeper and truer reality[14] at each step.

[14] Hume, in his famous sketch of the Human Understanding, makes all the perceptions of the human mind resolve themselves into two distinct kinds: *impressions* and *ideas*. "The difference between them consists in the degrees of force and liveliness with which they strike upon the mind, and make their way into our thought and consciousness. Those perceptions which enter with the most force and violence we may name *impressions*, and under this name include all our sensations, passions, and emotions, as they make their first appearance in the soul. By *ideas*, I mean the faint images of these in thinking and reasoning." "The identity which we ascribe to the mind of man is only a fictitious one."

From this we see that his stand-point is that of "sensuous ideas," the first stage of reflection. The second or third stage of reflection, if consistent, would not admit the reality to be the object of sense-impressions, and the abstract ideas to be only "faint images." One who holds, like Herbert Spencer, that persistent force is the ultimate reality—"the sole truth, which transcends experience by underlying it"—ought to hold that the generalization which reaches the idea of unity of force is the truest and most adequate of thoughts. And yet Herbert Spencer holds substantially the doctrine of Hume, in the words: "We must predicate nothing of objects too great or too multitudinous to be mentally represented, or

Sense-ideas which look upon the world as a world of independent objects, do not cognize the world truly. The next step, abstract ideas, cognizes the world as a process of forces, and "things" are seen to be mere temporary equilibria in the interaction of forces; "each thing is a bundle of forces." But the concrete idea of the Persistent force sees a deeper and more permanent reality underlying particular forces. It is one ultimate force. In it all multiplicity of existences has vanished, and yet it is the source of all particular existence.

This view of the world, on the stand-point of concrete idea, is pantheistic. It makes out a one supreme principle which originates and destroys all particular existences, all finite beings. It is the stand-point of Orientalism, or of the Asiatic thought. Buddhism and Brahminism have reached it, and not transcended it. It is a necessary stage of reflection in the mind, just as much as the stand-point of the first stage of reflection, which regards the world as composed of a multiplicity of independent things; or the stand-point of the second stage of reflection, which looks upon the world as a collection of relative existences in a state of process.

The final stand-point of the intellect is that in which it perceives the highest principle to be a self-determining or self-active Being, self-conscious, and creator of a world which manifests him. A logical investigation of the principle of "persistent force" would prove that this principle of Personal Being is presupposed as its true form. Since the "persistent force" is the sole and ultimate reality, it originates all other reality only by self-activity, and thus is self-determined. Self-determination implies self-consciousness as the true form of its existence.

These four forms of thinking, which we have arbitrarily called *sensuous*, *abstract*, *concrete*, and *absolute* ideas, correspond to four views of the world: (1) as a congeries of independent things; (2) as a play of forces; (3) as the evanescent appearance of a negative essential power; (4) as the creation of a Personal Creator, who makes it the theatre of the development of conscious beings in his image. Each step upward in ideas arrives at a more adequate idea of the true reality. *Force* is more real than *thing*; persistent force than particular forces; Absolute Person is more real than the force or forces which he creates.

---

we must make our predications by means of extremely inadequate representations of such objects—mere symbols of them." (Page 27 of "First Principles.")

This final form of thinking is the only form which is consistent with the theory of education. Each individual should ascend by education into participation—*conscious* participation—in the life of the species. Institutions—family, society, state, church—all are instrumentalities by which the humble individual may avail himself of the help of the race, and live over in himself its life. The highest stage of thinking is the stage of insight. It sees the world as explained by the principle of Absolute Person. It finds the world of institutions a world in harmony with such a principle.

SECOND DIVISION.

INTELLECTUAL EDUCATION OR DIDACTICS.

§ 80. *Mens sana in corpore sano* is correct as a maxim of pedagogics, though often false in the judgment of the empiric, for we do really sometimes find *mens sana in corpore insano* as well as *mens insana in corpore sano*, and yet all normal activity should strive to secure a true harmony of soul and body. The development of intelligence presupposes physical health. The science of the art of teaching is what we call didactics. As has already been said, it is conditioned first of all by orthobiotics; but, besides this, it depends in the sphere of mind on psychology and logic. In its process it must unite a careful consideration for psychology with a logical method.

First Chapter.

The Psychological Presupposition.

§ 81. If we would have any sound philosophy on this subject, we must, before we touch the subject of didactics, have examined somewhat closely the nature of mind itself, as it is unfolded in psychology. Any other treatment of the subject would be premature and ill-considered. We, therefore, take for granted some knowledge of those subjects on the part of our readers, as it would be out of place to unfold the entire subject in a treatise on pedagogics. We speak then of psychology only so far as is necessary to substantiate our propositions with regard to the educational work in hand, which is conditioned by it.

§ 82. The most important conception of all those taken from psychology is that of *attention*. Mind is essentially self-activity. What it does not make its own does not exist for it. We often speak as if something external did of itself make an impression on the mind, but this is never really the case. Nothing produces any effect on the mind, if the mind has not itself rendered itself receptive to it. Without this self-excited activity, the object produces no impression upon it, and it passes unaffected by it, because it has not been conscious of it. An illustration might here be drawn from medicine. The germs of disease do not affect that body which from its perfectly healthy activity offers no fruitful ground for their reception and growth; while the enfeebled or diseased organism welcomes them, and there they take root and grow. One man passes physically unconscious of danger through a plague-stricken city, while another is at once attacked because his body offers a welcoming ground for the all-present germs. It might also be illustrated in the moral world—one is unconscious of and untouched by evil, while another drinks it in. Every individual has his own horizon line of perception, which varies with his character and cultivation: As no two of us can ever see the same rainbow, or have precisely the same horizon; as no two can ever be conscious of precisely the same thoughts. This illustration may, however, perhaps mislead, for spirit does not exclude spirit as matter excludes matter. And, though we do exclude others from our material horizon, we need not necessarily exclude them from our spiritual horizon. Attention is the directing of the mind to a certain object of thought with the purpose of comprehending it in its unity and in its distinction from other objects. The mind voluntarily relinquishes its hold upon other objects for the time, in order to fix upon this one; and, if this essential, spontaneous activity of the mind be lacking, it gains absolutely nothing. All success in teaching and learning depends upon the clearness and strength with which we distinguish objects and thoughts from each other. If, as the old Latin proverb[15] implies, he who does not distinguish clearly does not teach well, it is as true that he who cannot draw clear distinctions well cannot learn.

§ 83. Since the art of attention depends on the self-determination of the person, it can be fostered, and the pupil can be made attentive by his teacher. Education must accustom him to a sharp, quick, and many-sided attention, so that he shall gain by his first examination of the object of attention an exact and true idea of it, and shall not be obliged to make repeated efforts to acquire this. We must have no patience with that half-attention, that sort

[15] Bene qui distinguit, bene docet.

of twilight and half-light of intelligence in which one is obliged to correct and re-correct his first impression, because the attention was not sufficiently awake to make that first impression correct.

Nothing is of more vital importance to the teacher than to be convinced that it is his business to create and to cultivate the habit of close attention, and to know that, if his pupils are not attentive, it is his own fault: It is his business to make them so. That is what his vocation means, and, when he has done this, he might almost be said to have done his work. But how often we hear teachers speaking of their pupils as inattentive in much the same way as they might say, "Poor boy, he is humpbacked!" as if want of attention were a natural deficiency for which allowance was to be made. Make a child thoroughly attentive to what you say to him at all times, and show him where to go for mental food, and your work is done. All that is then wanting, time will accomplish. It is the teacher's essential business to make his pupils attentive, and, if he fail here, he fails as a teacher, whatever else he may be.

§ 84. We must never forget the principle of psychology, that the mind does not consist of a bundle of faculties as a collection of different powers, but that all which it does proceeds from different activities of the one and identical subject. They are all a part of his very nature, so that education must not omit to foster and strengthen them all. It is quite correct to say, according to the old principle *a potiori fit denominatio*, that man is distinguished from brutes by his power of thinking, and also by his power of will mediated through thought; but we must never forget that to be a perfect man he must also possess feeling and imagination. The special directions which the cognizing intelligence may take in its activity are: (1) Perception or Observation; (2) Conception or Representation; (3) Thinking. These are all interwoven and interdependent, and thus act by and through each other. Perception does not, however, only rise into conception, or conception into thinking; but thinking returns into conception, and conception into perception. We might say that in the infant the perceptive faculty is most active; in the child the conceptive, and in the youth the thinking faculty; and then we might with some reason distinguish here in the development of the youth an intuitive, an imaginative, and a logical period.

Serious errors arise if we do not carefully observe these different elements, and the way in which they are actively related to each other, and if we confuse the different forms in which they appear in the different stages of growth. The child thinks, while he perceives, but his thinking is as it were concealed from him, because it is unconscious; and when he has acquired perceptions he makes them into conceptions, and demonstrates to himself his own freedom by playing with them; his play must not be looked upon as simply enjoyment. The child in play is occupied in trying the various perceptions which his consciousness has accumulated, by his own self-determination and by his power of idealizing—i. e., he has gathered material for use. Now he takes a pleasure in establishing the fact that he is the master of this material, and not it of him. He will do with it what he, the master, pleases; a board shall be a ship, the grass the ocean; anything shall be what he wills it to be. We do not mean that the child consciously tries the validity of his perception-material as against his will, but he does it unconsciously, and his most enjoyable plays have the most of this element in them. The stories that children most like are those that have most of the miraculous. All these stories transgress the narrow limits of actuality, and their caprice is not attractive to the abstract understanding, which would rather present to the children the commonplace tales of "Charitable Ann," "Heedless Frederick," or "Inquisitive Wilhelmina." It praises above all "Robinson Crusoe," which, while it relates curious and uncommon things, yet contains nothing which is absolutely impossible. But the desire of the child, wiser than the schools, laughs these to scorn, and revels in impossibilities—"Jack the Giant-Killer," "Puss in Boots," the "Arabian Nights," and all sorts of delicious fairy fancies; and thus, and only thus, it grows healthily into youth, where, with the assuming of the earnest duties of life, imagination grows less vivid, and the understanding and reason come to the helm.

I. The Intuitive Epoch.

§ 85. Perception, the first act of intellectual culture, is the unfettered grasping by the mind of an object which is directly present to it. According to this definition, education can have nothing to do with the act, because the act must be entirely uninfluenced from without, and the mind be left to its own innate power. It can only render aid so that the grasping may be more easy, i. e., 1. It can isolate the object which is to be apprehended. 2. It can facilitate the transition from one to another. 3. It can call attention to varied points of interest, so that the return to an object once examined may not become wearisome or monotonous, but have an ever-fresh charm. Here, at the very beginning, comes in for the teacher the principle of repetition which is one of his main tools, and the necessity of making that necessary repetition so varied in its aspects as never to weary the pupil by monotony. Lacking the ingenuity necessary to do this last, any one might as well decide to embrace some other calling than that of teacher. The way in which one amuses an infant illustrates the helps which education may offer to the art of perception. We hold up a ball, i. e., 1. We isolate it from the mass of surrounding objects in which it was lost; 2. We transfer the interest from the ball to the string which holds it, or to its own motion as we roll or toss it; 3. We call attention to its color or size or softness.

§ 86. But, direct perception of many things is impossible from their extent or distance, and yet it is necessary that we have perception of many things, and, therefore, we make use of pictures to enlarge the field of the sense of sight. But we cannot have many objects represented at their actual size, and this implies the necessity of a reduced scale of measure, and this again implies some need of care that the representation may not convey to the mind an idea of too large or too small a real object. To the picture, then, explanation must be added.

§ 87. The picture is a wonderful aid to the teacher when it is correct and characteristic. Especially those pictures should be correct which represent natural objects or historical persons or scenes. If they are not correct, it is better not to use them, as they will do no good even if they do not do harm.

Picture-books seem to have been first used as a means of instruction in the second half of the seventeenth century, or after the decay of the art of painting, and to have followed from miniature painting. Up to that time public life was more given to the picturesque in its arms, furniture, houses, and churches, and people were more weary of actual seeing because they led a constantly wandering life. After this time, when, in the fury of the Thirty Years' War, all arts of painting and sculpture and the Christian and Pagan mythology had died out, there began to be felt a need of picture representations. The *Orbis rerum sensualium pictus*, which was to be also *Janua linguarum reserata*, appeared in 1658 and was reprinted in 1805. It has been followed by a mass of illustrated books on all subjects. The historical illustrated books were divided into two classes: Biblical and secular. These are in countless numbers, but most of them very poor. It is deplorable to see what daubs are put into the hands of children. They are not wanting in high color but in correctness, to say nothing of character, they are good for nothing, and the most annoying thought about them is that for the same money and with the same labor something quite different could have been produced with a little application of conscientiousness and scientific knowledge. The uniformity in the books offered in our stores is really disgraceful. Everywhere are presented to us the same types, especially in the ethnographic department. How much better would it be if, in representing the Hindoo nation, we were shown types of the four castes which have conditioned the history of the nation! Instead of this, we have perhaps a picture of a dancer. In natural history we have too often the representations of some imaginative artist, or the drawing of some miserable specimen. But there are signs of improvement here. In architectural drawings and in landscapes much has already been done.

§ 88. Children seem to have a natural desire to collect specimens—such as plants, butterflies, beetles, shells, skeletons, etc.,—and this desire can be strengthened and directed so that their powers of perception shall gain in exactness and vividness. They ought especially to be practised in drawing, so that they can make good copies from the real objects. Drawing in schools is not to be regarded so much as a practice in art as a means of educating the sight so that the child may judge somewhat correctly of distance, size, and color, and if he can be thus led by carefully graded lessons to a knowledge of the elementary forms of nature, he will have gained a power which will, in many ways, both theoretical and practical, be of great service to him.

Although we should not expect much æsthetic effect from pictures given as illustrations, inasmuch as the child must concentrate his attention on the distinguishing features of form and color rather than on the harmony of the whole and the style of execution, yet we should never omit to give children some idea of what true art is. If real works of art are to be found in the neighborhood, we can trust to the power which these will exercise over the child, and we must patiently await their moral and æsthetic effect. Our American children are greatly at a disadvantage in this matter in comparison with the children in any European capital, for we have none of the art treasures either in painting, sculpture, or architecture, which must have so powerful an influence on the children brought up in their atmosphere. The art of photography in its various forms will, in some degree, assist us here. As it is certainly the study of the human spirit and its manifestations, and not the study of the works of nature, which has the greatest humanizing and developing effect upon our minds, we should make every effort to bring the study of art to bear on the child's mind.

§ 89. But the study of pictures may become only a means of mental dissipation without any gain to the mind if it be not accompanied by explanation. Pictures are not instructive in and by themselves. They must be interpreted by means of human thought: the mere looking at them is utterly valueless. The tendency in our time is now to amuse children by looking simply, and to avoid all real effort of hard thinking. But as Gladstone remarks: There has as yet been no way found to make attention and inattention equal in their results. It is not alone the thing in itself that we want. We must go behind the thing itself for a knowledge which shall not be merely empty and useless. But illustrations are the order of the day, and in the place of enjoyable descriptions we often find only miserable pictures. We can reach beyond mere things in order to gain a comprehension of their real nature, only and solely by the power of hard thinking. The danger of Kindergartens lies exactly here. If they turn out children with an utterly dissipated habit of mind and with an insatiate desire to be amused, they have done the children irretrievable harm. But in good hands the Kindergarten may prove the best means for the correction of thoughtless, unsystematic mental activity.

§ 90. The ear as well as the eye must be cultivated. But, while we must look at music as an educational means, we must not forget its ethical influence. Hearing is the most internal of our senses, and is, therefore, to be treated with the greatest care. Especially should the child be led to consider speech, not merely as a means by which he can obtain the gratification of his desires and make his thoughts known, but as a something from which real pleasure is to be derived in itself. He should be taught to speak distinctly and expressively, and this is possible only through a higher degree of care and deliberation. Nothing is more neglected in English-speaking schools than a proper study of the mother tongue. Matthew Arnold has recorded this in his "Report on the Schools of the Continent" with regard to English schools, in comparison with those of Germany and France, and the criticism would have applied to American schools as well. American voices are not good, therefore they should be treated with special care. The high and shallow tones should be lowered and deepened, and this can be done in our schools. And with regard to the language itself, it should be made an object of special exercise and study from the earliest school years. That time would not be wasted which was given daily to a conversation exercise in which the pupils should be led to express their own ideas correctly in their own language; at any rate, it should be a teacher's constant duty to demand and enforce the use of pure and correct English in every word spoken in school.

The Greek nation gave the greatest care to the musical[16] education of their youth. We find the evidence of this set down with the greatest clearness in the Republic of Plato, and in the last book of Aristotle's Politics. With modern nations also, music occupies a large share of attention, and is a constant element of education. Pianoforte playing is very general, and singing is also much practised; but the ethical significance of music is sometimes overlooked. It is too often considered as a means for social display only, and the selections played are of an exciting or even bacchanalian character. This style greatly excites youthful nerves. But speech, the highest form of personal manifestation of the mind, was treated with the greatest veneration and respect by the ancient world. We moderns write and read so much that the art of speaking clearly, correctly, and agreeably has much degenerated, and we do not gain any compensation for this loss by the art of modern so-called "declamation." We are left to hope for an improvement in this respect by means of the greater freedom of speech which now prevails in our political and religious life.

II. The Imaginative Epoch.

§ 91. Through our forms of perception, aided by reflection, we gain mental pictures which the mind has the power of summoning at will at any time, and in the absence of the object which originally produced them. This power we call imagination. The mental picture may be (1) exactly like the perception which originally gave rise to it; or (2) it may be at its pleasure changed and combined with other pictures; or (3) it may be held in the form of abstract signs or symbols, which the mind in vents for it. Thus we have the powers of (1) the recognition of perceptions; (2) of the creative imagination, and (3) memory; but, for the full development of these subjects, we must turn to psychology.

§ 92. (1) The mental picture which we sketch from an object may be a correct one, or it may be imperfect, or very faulty, according as we have

[16] "Music," with the Greeks, included what we should call belles-lettres—the arts over which the nine Muses presided—not only music proper, but rhetoric, poetry, and the drama and stage presentation.

observed it without prejudice as it properly exists; or as we have beheld it accidentally confused with other objects, and have thought its qualities to be essential, which were really only accidental at the time of observation. Education must form a habit of comparing the observations which we make with our conceptions, in order to distinguish in the object those qualities which are essential and really belong to it from those which are accidental, and, therefore, foreign. On this critical examination depends the correctness of our conceptions.

§ 93. (2) Our conceptions are to an extent limited by the material found for them in our previous perceptions, but we exercise a perfectly free control over the combination or altering of them. We can at our will create out of these elements innumerable pictures, and these we do not recognize as anything presented to us from outside, but as our own creation. This is a pleasurable action of the mind, but it is not as a mere pleasure that the science of education has to consider it. The student of education sees the reaction which our power of idealizing sets up against the limits necessarily fixed by our receiving chance impressions from without, and the conditions under which we can reproduce them by means of our creative imagination. Thus we do not paint for ourselves merely the actually existing world, but we create for ourselves and out of ourselves a new world of our own.

§ 94. This faculty is most surely and most easily cultivated by means of poetry, which pedagogics must therefore employ as a valuable means. The imagination must learn to appreciate what is good taste here by a study of the classical works of the creative imagination in this field. And for youth the classical works are those which nations have produced in their early or childish periods. These works present to the mind of the child the picture of the world which the human mind in the necessary stages of its development was forced to sketch out for itself. This is the real reason why children never tire of the stories of Homer, or of the Old Testament. Polytheism and the heroism which belongs to it are as real elements of childish imagination as monotheism and its prophets and patriarchs. Our view is above and beyond both, because it really contains them both as elements, while it comes to us by means of both of them.

The most genuine stories for children, from seven to fourteen, are always the same: those which are always to be honored as an inheritance from the nation and the world. For example, we can not fail to notice in how many thousand forms the stories of Ulysses have been reproduced as tales for children. Becker's "Tales of Ancient Times;" Gustav Schwab's beautiful "Stories of the Olden Time;" Karl Grimm's "Old Stories," etc., what were they if deprived of the legend of the silver-tongued wily favorite of Pallas and the divine Swineherd? The stories. of the Old Testament up to the separation of Judah and Israel are equally inexhaustible. These patriarchs with their wives and daughters, these judges and prophets, these kings and priests, are made nothing but models of virtue by the slip-shod morality which would strike out everything hard or uncouth from the books which it prepares for "our dear children." Precisely because the dark side of human nature is not wanting, because envy, vanity, evil desire, ingratitude, craftiness, and deceit are found among the fathers and leaders of the "chosen people of God" have these stories so great an educational value. Adam, Cain, Abraham, Joseph, Samson, and David are as truly world-historical types as Achilles and Patroclus, Agamemnon and Iphigenia, Hector and Andromache, Ulysses and Penelope.

§ 95. Each nation and people has in the primitive epochs of its own history enough material for pictures which will fill the imagination of children, and will make familiar to them the characteristic traits of the past of their own people.

The Germans have a great number of such stories. Such are the "Horn-covered Siegfried," the "Heymon Children," the "Beautiful Magelone," "Fortunatus," the "Wandering Jew," "Faust," the "Adventurous Simplicissimus," the "Schildbürger," the "Island of Felsenburg," "Lienhard and Gertrude," etc., etc. Also the art-works of the great masters which have a national significance must be included, as, e. g., the "Don Quixote" of Cervantes. Such books as these should be left where the children will find them and pick them up. They should not be urged to read them, but allowed to come on them, as it were by chance. They will not absorb what in them may be coarse, but they will gain a somewhat of health and nobleness from them, and a taste for such food as will make them turn away with disgust from the sensational so-called children's stories of the present day. Of those which it were desirable for children to read in English, for instance, are Swift's "Gulliver's Travels," Lamb's "Essays," "Don Quixote," Cooper's novels, Scott's novels, "Arabian Nights," Johnson's "Voyage to the Hebrides," etc., etc., Homer and Virgil in rhymed translations. They will not read much of Lamb's "Essays," and yet, after all, they will get a flavor from them which will be a good influence for them.

§ 96. The most general form in which the imagination of children finds exercise is that of fairy stories. Education must see to it, however, that these are the genuine stories, the product of a nation's thought, and not in the form in which modern poets have sometimes dressed them up, and which are really only frightful caricatures.

The fairy stories of India are really at the head here, since they proceed from a nation of children, as it were, who lived almost wholly in the imagination. As we have them given to us through the Arabians in the time of the caliphs, they have lost their exclusively Indian character, and have become, in the tales of Scheherezade, a book whose fame is as broad as the world, and with which no local traditions, as, e. g., Grimm's collection of German stories, though they are indeed admirable, can in any wise compare.

The stories which have been written especially for the improvement of children, which are full of moral teachings and hints, are very repulsive to the liberty-loving imagination of children. They do not have the true ring in them. We must acknowledge, however, that there seems to be some improvement in this respect, since we have learned the difference between the natural poetry of a people, which is perfectly artless and not reflective, and poetry which is conditioned and limited by criticism and an ideal. Even the picture-books of children show symptoms of improvement. We do not have so often now those useless books in which the letters of the alphabet, highly colored, form the chief attraction. But such writers as Hofman, who gave us "Slovenly Peter" have shown that even seemingly trivial things can be treated with genius, provided one is blessed with it, and that nothing is more opposed to the imagination of the child than *childishness*, an effort after which has ruined so many would-be authors of books for children. They have attempted to come down with dignity from their own lofty standpoint, and have fallen into the bottomless pit of inanity, and the children have spurned their works as they deserved. We have begun to understand that, when Christ promised the kingdom of heaven to little children, it was possibly for other reasons than because they had, as it were, the privilege of being thoughtless and foolish.

Hans Christian Andersen in our day has given us a perfect specimen of what genuine children's stories are; and Lewis Carroll has also nearly, but not quite, approached him in his "Alice in Wonderland," and "Through the Looking-Glass," in which the unchecked fancy is allowed to run perfectly wild, as it does in the mind of a healthy child. But too many of our "Children's

Magazine" writers fall into the error of supposing that stories about children are necessarily stories for children.

§ 97. As the child grows towards manhood, the stories given to him should take on more of the earnest character of real lite, and imagination must yield to reality. We must learn to look on the world no longer as an aimless play, but as it really is, a genuine battle. In the place of the entrancing epic poem he must now be given tragedy, which will, through sensations of fear and pity, present to him human destiny with all its darker shadows of sin and atonement. Biography now becomes of value in the department of history, such as Plutarch's "Lives" in ancient history, and in modern, the autobiographies of Augustine, Cellini, Rousseau, Goethe, Varnhagen, Jung Stilling, Moritz Arndt, etc. In these autobiographies the youth can see how the individual characters grew as they came in contact with surrounding circumstances, how they were influenced by these, and how these in turn influenced them. These, as well as memoirs and letters of distinguished men, are of great use to the youth who, by studying the battles of others, thus learns how he shall best fight his own. He will learn to know nature and ethnography by means of volumes of travels, which will make him a sharer in the charm and joy of the first discovery, and this is a much more delightful possession than the mere general consciousness of the results of the achievements of the race.

But, while we thus widen the horizon of knowledge of facts by instructive literature, we must not omit, at the same time, to secure wider views of the realm of ideas. This we can do best by what we shall call philosophical literature. Of this there are only two kinds to be recommended: (1) well-written treatises which endeavor by a thorough treatment to solve the conditions of some single problem, and (2), when the mind is strong enough, some standard works of philosophy. German literature is especially rich in works of this kind, as those of Lessing, Herder, Kant, Fichte, Schleiermacher, Humboldt, and Schiller. Nothing hurts the mind of a youth more than the study of works of mediocrity, or those of a still lower grade. Nay, they even devastate, spoil, and narrow his powers of appreciative feeling by their empty, hollow, and constrained style. People are apt to say that the real classical works are too hard, and that the student must approach these by means of those of less depth and difficulty. This is a wide-spread and most dangerous error, because these so-called Introductions, Explanatory Essays, Easy Expositions, Comprehensive Abstracts, are very much more difficult to understand—for the reason that they lack all originality and all sharply-drawn distinctions—than the classical works to which they pretend to open an approach. Education must inspire the youth with courage to attack the real classics, and must never allow him to think (as a discretion born of prejudice will often tell him) that he cannot understand such works as Fichte's "Science of Knowledge," Aristotle's "Metaphysics," and Hegel's "Phenomenology." No science suffers so much as philosophy from this false popular opinion, which understands neither itself nor its authority. The youth must *learn how to learn to understand*, and to this end he must know that all things cannot be understood at first glance, but that there are ideas so valuable and life-giving as to demand that he have patience, that he read over and over again, and then that he think over what he has read.

§ 98. (3) The imagination is always going back into perception for the materials out of which to create its images. These perceptions may have some resemblance to the perception which lies at the root of the conception, in which case they are more or less symbolic, or they may be only arbitrary creations of the imagination, and then they are pure signs. The voluntary holding fast of one of these perceptions created by the imagination, the recalling of the conceptions denoted by them, we generally call *Memory*. This is not a special power which the mind has of recalling things, e.g., names or persons or dates. But, properly speaking, memory is as to its form the stage of annulment of the mental image; as to its content, it arises from the interest which we take in a subject. When we are very much interested in anything, we give it on that account a very careful attention, and if we give it a careful attention the reproductive imagination can easily recall it. These states of the mind being given, the fixing of a name or of a date which relates to the action in which the mind was so absorbed presents no difficulty. When the interest and attention are so vivid, it seems that no effort is needed to impress the memory. All so-called mnemonic aids only make more instead of less difficult the act of memory. This is in itself a double action, consisting of (1) the fixing of the sign, and (2) of the conception which rests upon it. But a mnemonic sign adds yet another conception by means of which the data about whose memory we were concerned shall be more firmly held, and since this is arbitrary we add another stage to memory which is already twofold. We must first recall the sign, however arbitrary or artificial it may be, and then also its relation to the thing we wish to remember. To be of any real help to the memory, we must not try to help it at all. We must simply place the object clearly before the mind in the presence of the infinite power of the self-determination, which is the prerogative of mind.

It will thus be seen of how immense importance is the cultivation of the power of attention which has been before spoken of. All the teaching in the world will do no good if the attention is not vividly excited, if the child has not attained the power of self-control, self-management, by which he can at once and steadily give his attention to any required subject. And if this power has been acquired, then the teacher has nothing to do but simply to place the object in the focus of these rays of attention, and it will be firmly memorized, even without voluntary effort on the part of the pupil. The problem of instruction is thus perfectly simple. First teach the child control over his own mind, and then simply lay before him what you wish him to make his own.

Lists of names, as, e. g., of the Roman emperors, of the popes, of the caliphs, of rivers, mountains, authors, cities, etc., also numbers, as, e. g., the multiplication table, the melting-points of minerals, the dates of battles, of births and deaths, etc., must be learned without aid. All indirect means only make the matter more difficult. We should use them only when the interest or attention has been weakened, and they should then be invented by each one for himself.

§ 99. We can fix information in the memory by pronouncing and writing down the names and dates, and then by constant repetition. By the first means we can gain exactness, and by the second, certainty.

There is no artificial contrivance which aids the memory like writing down what we wish to remember, always provided that we do not write simply for the purpose of relieving the memory of its proper work. It is, so far as we are concerned, a mere matter of chance that a name or a number should be thus or so; we cannot change it, and must thus learn it as it is, if it is worth learning at all, but there is no reason in it, and it calls for no exercise of intelligence.

In science proper, as, e. g., in philosophy, our reason helps us to distinguish the meaning by the connection, and the names have a reason for them, so that we should invent them for ourselves if they were not already invented.

III. The Logical Epoch.

§ 100. In conception the mind attains a sort of universality, for it is not bounded or limited by any definite present object, and the accidental details can be brought into some classification or *schema*, to use Kant's expression. But the *necessity* of the connection of these details is wanting. To produce this is the work of the thought which can free itself from all figurative forms, and with its simple determinations transcend the conceptions. This thought purifies itself in its process of conception and perception; notion, judgment, and syllogism, develop into forms which, as such, have no power of being perceived by the senses. It must not, however, be understood that the thinking person cannot pass out of the region of thought and carry it with him back again into that of conception and perception. Genuine thinking activity shuts itself out of no sphere, and deprives itself of no content. That abstraction which affects a logical purism and looks scornfully down on the regions of conception and perception as forms of intelligence quite inferior to itself, is a false thinking, a sickly error of scholasticism. Education will guard itself against such an error, in proportion as it has carefully led the pupil by the established road of intellectual development to thinking, through the paths of perception and conception. Thus memorizing is an excellent preparatory school for the thinking activity, as it gives exercise to the intelligence in dealing with abstract ideas.

§ 101. The surest way of leading the child into the power to think is carefully from his earliest years to foster the *sense of truth*. If we can teach him to give himself up unreservedly and freely to truth when it is presented to him, and to form a habit of diligently hunting out and exposing error and false appearance, we shall have done the greatest thing toward producing strength of the reflective powers. He will then not be liable to be deceived into accepting anything less than the true and genuine connection and dependence of thought in other ways.

[This is one of the places where Rosencranz touches in a masterly way upon the principle that true intellectual and true moral instruction cannot be dissevered. The teacher who demands from his pupils always the exact statement of the facts they have to give and requires them to seek for and expose the false, who creates in them the habit of thoroughness in their intellectual work, is doing more for them in a moral way, though he never says a definite word upon the abstract subject of truthfulness, than he who delivers long lessons upon its necessity while he allows careless and superficial work in himself or his pupils, and does not show himself willing and eager to acknowledge his own errors. This demand for the truth, the whole truth, and nothing but the truth, in lessons, is the most important moral lesson which can be given to our youth, and will bear the most plentiful harvest. This is a most fruitful thought for the student who is to be a teacher.]

An illusion as a pleasing play of the intelligence is quite allowable, but a lie is never to be tolerated. Children like to mystify and to be mystified. They like to pretend to tease and to act another part than their own. This inclination toward some kind of illusion is perfectly normal with them, and, therefore, to be encouraged. It gives ground for the glorious kingdom of art and the poetry of conversation which is jest and wit, and this, although often stereotyped into prosaic conventional forms, is preferable to the clumsy honesty which takes everything in its simple, literal sense. It is easy to discover when children in such play, in the activity of their joyousness, incline to the side of disorder and confusion, by their showing a selfish interest in it. Then they must be stopped, for the delight of harmless artifice degenerates into crafty premeditation and dissimulation.

§ 102. The study of the logical forms is doubtless a special pedagogical help in the logical training of the intelligence. Practice in mathematics is not sufficient, because it presupposes logic. Mathematics is related to logic in the same way as grammar, physics, etc. But these logical forms must be presented in their pure independence, and not implicitly in their objective form as propositions.

ANALYSIS[17] AND COMMENTARY.

BY WILLIAM T. HARRIS.

Education is the development of reason innate in man—theoretical as intellect, practical as will-power. It is a labor that changes an ideal into a real, making what is potential into an actual; transfiguring the "natural" man, so to speak, into a spiritual man. Education forms "habits." It develops ideal human nature into real human nature by means of this formation of habits. (Play differs from Labor in this, that it does not seek to transform an ideal into a real, but to make a semblance of contradiction between the ideal and real; it makes a reality *seem* to be what it is not.) There are three special elements in man, each of which needs education: these are life (bodily organism), cognition (knowing faculty or intellect), and will. To some extent there is a succession of periods based on this distinction: (1) the period of nurture, lasting till the sixth year, or during infancy, in which the education of the body is more important than the education of the mind; (2) the period of the school, lasting through childhood—say to fourteen years—in which *general* or intellectual education is most important; (3) the period of youth—from fourteen to eighteen—in which the most important education is specializing the practical application of knowledge and strength to particular forms of duty, hence will-education. While these periods are thus distinguished by the relative importance of the three different disciplines, it is essential that no one of these disciplines shall be neglected in any period.

§ 52. The classification in pedagogics is based on the distinction of the three elements in man that require education. (1) Physical (correct living = orthobiotics); (2) intellectual (correct perceiving, knowing, and thinking = didactics); (3) practical (correct action, proper habits = pragmatics).

[17] This contains also additional reflections, often substituted in place of analysis where the text is clear without restatement.

Æsthetic training, or the sense for the appreciation and production of the beautiful, falls, in a threefold division, into the second—into theoretic education. Social, moral, and religious training belong to the third division, as they concern the will and its utterance in deeds. "Pragmatics" signifies the doctrine of human deeds, and includes the spheres of ethics, politics, and religion. There may be defined a fivefold system of education, basing the distinction on the institutions of civilization: (a) Nurture = the education of the family; (b) the school, or education into the conventionalities of intelligence; (c) the art, trade, or profession that forms the vocation in life = the education of civil society; (d) the political education into citizenship, resulting from obedience to laws and participation in making and sustaining them; (e) religious education. These five forms of education depend on (a) the family, (b) the school, (c) civil society, (d) the State, (e) the Church. The school is properly a transition between the family and civil society, and forms the institution of education *par excellence*. Hence, while education, very properly, is defined so as to include all of human life, there is a period specially characterized as "education" which transpires in the school, a special institution that partakes of the character of the family on the one hand, and of civil society on the other. In the school, of course, there should be some attention paid to all spheres of education, but its main business should be the acquisition "of the picture of the world such as mature minds through experience and insight have painted it" (see § 51 near the end), or, in other words, those conventional items of information, insights into laws and principles, and the elementary processes of their combination. This makes the "view of the world" which each civilized human being is supposed to possess. It is important to know the exact province of the school, and to see that it is only one of the five forms of education that civilization provides for man. Much of the carping criticism leveled against schools, in times of financial distress or general social depression, is based on the assumption that the province of the school is *all* education instead of a small, but very important, fraction of it. The school may do its share of correct education, but it cannot correct the effects of neglect of family nurture, nor insure its youth against evil that will follow if civil society furnishes no steady employment, no opportunity for settled industry, and the State no training into consciousness of higher manhood by its just laws, and by offering to the citizen a participation in the political process of legislation and administration, carefully guarding its forms so that its politics does not furnish a training in corruption. Nor can the school insure the future of its pupils unless the Church does its part in the education of the individuals of the community. "The scientific arrangement of these ideas"—*i. e.*, life, intellect, and will—"must show that the former, as more abstract, constitute the conditions"—*i. e.*, life is the condition of intellect, and both intellect and life the conditions of will—while "the latter, as more concrete, are the ground of the former" *i. e.*, intellect is the ground of life, or, in other words, its final cause, and so will is the ground and final cause of intellect. Intellect contains all that life contains, and much more, namely: While life realizes its totality of species only in many individuals, and each individual is a partial and special half of the species as male or female, the intellect as consciousness is subject and object in one, and each individual intellect is potentially the entire species—each thinking being can think all the thoughts of the greatest thinkers. So, will contains all that intellect contains, and more. For what is potential in intellect (the identity of subject and object of thought) is real in the will. The will makes objective its internal subjective forms, and in its highest ethical activity it becomes conscious freedom.

§ 53. The rules of hygiene are derived from an insight into the twofold process of assimilation and elimination which goes on in the living organism with relation to the inorganic substances which it uses.

§ 54. Perpetual change goes on in the living organism, converting the inorganic into organic tissue and then reconverting it. This alternation is the basis of the demand for the alternation of productive activity with rest and recreation in the whole physical system.

§ 55. Fatigue defined. It may occur with the whole organism or with a part. The idea that total rest is healthy is a misapprehension. The organism requires alternation of rest and activity, which alternation itself is activity because it is change. Hence, "true strength arises only from activity."

§ 56. Physical education treats of (a) the repairing activity or nutrition, (b) the motor or muscular activity, and (c) the nervous activity, as far as they concern children and youth.

§ 57. Dietetics defined. Details here are trivial.

§§ 58, 59, 60, 61. Food for infants.

§ 62. Why children need much sleep.

§ 63. Clothing of children should allow free play of the limbs, and not compress the vital organs. Its clothing should not be a source of anxiety to the child, nor the occasion of vanity or of humiliation.

§ 64. Cleanliness means "a place for every thing and every thing in its place." To take a thing out of its proper relations is to "deprive it of its proper individuality," and in an "elemental chaos" every thing has lost its proper relations to other things, and has no longer any use or fitness in its existence.

§ 65. *Gymnastics.* The voluntary and involuntary muscles distinguished—the former depend on the brain direct, while the latter depend on the spinal cord; the voluntary muscles form the means of communication with the external world, and also react on the automatic functions of digestion, sensation, etc. Gymnastics seeks to develop the voluntary muscles in a normal manner, and through these indirectly to affect favorably the development of the other bodily systems and processes.

§ 66. Gymnastics affected by the national military drill. The ancient tribes and nations found special bodily training indispensable to success in war, and even to national preservation. Gunpowder and the improved arms that use it have almost rendered gymnastics obsolete—the successful army, other things equal, being the one composed of men thoroughly disciplined in manœuvres, and possessed individually of tact and versatility necessary to manipulate the destructive fire-arms now used.

§ 67. Gymnastics, therefore, in modern times must aim chiefly at developing the body for the sake of physical strength and endurance, with a view to the demands of useful industry and mental culture on the bodily health and vigor. Health requires harmonious development; the exercises must develop the parts of the body so as not to produce disproportion. The result of gymnastics is to give the mind control over the body as a whole—the will interpenetrates, as it were, the various organs, and by this means the conscious mind can reenforce the automatic functions of the body; the will-power can to a certain degree even ward off disease.

§§ 68-71. Gymnastic exercises classified: (1) of the lower extremities: (a) walking, (b) running, (c) leaping (including varieties and modifications, such as walking on stilts, skating, dancing, balancing, etc.); (2) of the upper extremities: (a) lifting, (b) swinging, (c) throwing—(including also the modifications of climbing, carrying, pole and bar exercises, quoits, ball and nine-pin playing, etc.); (3) of the whole body: (a) swimming, (b) riding, (c) fighting.

§ 72. The gradation of exercises chronologically corresponds in some degree with their classification—(a) walking, running, leaping, to infancy; (b) lifting, swinging, throwing, to childhood; (c) swimming, riding, bodily contests, to youth, and to manhood so far as manhood continues athletic sports. The period of sexual development begins with youth, and needs special attention at the hand of the educator.

§ 73. Great care must be exercised in the period of youth as to food—its regularity, and proper quality and amount; the physical exercise, too, must be strictly observed. These precautions may prevent a premature diversion of the nervous power of the body to a manifestation of the sexual instinct.

§ 74. There must be no overstraining of the brain or morbid excitement of the feelings in the period of youth, if we would have a healthful development of the sexual instinct. Novel-reading should be carefully limited as to amount and character.

§ 80. Education has to note bodily conditions of the mind, and to prescribe methods of physical training. It has more especially to note also the nature of mind, or psychology, and prescribe the methods of developing the several powers of the mind.

§ 81. Psychology, as a science, is unfolded within the philosophy of spirit as an antecedent presupposition of the science of ethics (which forms the third part of the science of spirit, see "Analysis" § 1, page 38, of this work). Hence pedagogics, which belongs to ethics (or social science), presupposes psychology, and refers to it as already established. Pedagogics, in treating of intellectual education, may give only an outline of it.

§ 82. The conception of attention—the most important one in pedagogics. Nothing exists for the mind unless the mind gives attention to it—*i. e.*, voluntarily entertains it. [Attention is self-activity, not a passivity of the mind. It is the will acting upon the intellect, and hence a combination of intellect and will. Out of the infinitely manifold objects before the senses—and each object is capable of endless subdivision, there is no part so small that it does not possess variety and the possibility of further subdivision—attention selects one special field or province, and refuses to be diverted from it. It neglects all else and returns again and again from the borders of the field of attention, and takes note of the relation of the surrounding objects to the object of special attention. It makes it the essential thing, and considers every thing else only as related to it.]

[It is interesting to note how the higher faculties (*so-called* "faculties"—one must not, however, suppose these faculties as isolated "properties" of the mind, existing side by side, like properties of a thing) all originate from the process of attention; they are higher powers or "potencies" of attention. Isaac Newton ascribed his superiority to other men in intellectual power simply to the greater power of attention. Attention appears: *first*, as a mere power of isolating one object from others—a power of concentration upon it to the exclusion of others; *secondly*, it discriminates distinctions within the object or *analyzes* it: thus analysis is continued attention—the second power or potence of attention; *thirdly*, it seizes again upon one of the distinctions found by analysis, and becomes *abstraction*; abstraction might be named the third power or potence of attention; *fourthly*, the attention may be directed to essential relations of the elements formed by analysis and abstraction—their essential relations to each other. This is a process of synthetic thought, a grasping-together, a comprehension—a higher activity of mind—a fourth potence or power of attention. It is the most important matter in psychology, this process of synthesis, through necessary relation. To find that one object of attention, A, involves another, B—possesses essential relation to it, such that A cannot exist without B—is to find a necessary synthesis. It is to discover that instead of A by itself, or B by itself, there is one existence having two phases to it, one phase being A, and the other phase being B. It is a finding of one instead of two, and is a synthetic act of mind. The synthesis is not an arbitrary one. It is a discovery of truth—A and B were really two aspects of one and the same being which we may call A B, but they *seemed* to be independent. The process of attention, up to its fourth power, is thus an ascent from *seeming* to *being*. The perception of *dependence* ("essential relation" is *dependence*) is the perception of synthesis, and belongs to the activity of *comprehension*. Reflection, as a mental activity (or "faculty"), is the process of discovering relations and dependencies among objects—hence it is a stage of synthesis—belonging to what we call here the "fourth power of attention." The student of educational psychology should follow out this mode of exploring the mind, and define for himself all of the so-called "faculties" and mental acts, in terms of attention (see the Outline of Educational Psychology, especially VI). He must note, too, that the act of attention is an act of the mind, directed upon itself because it *confines* its own activity (*i. e.*, the perception in general) to a special field (*i. e.*, makes it perception of a special object to the exclusion of others). This synthesis is, as just remarked, the most important theme of psychology—it is also the most wonderful—a veritable fountain of surprise. For the strangest thing to learn in psychology is that the process of reflection (the direction of the mind in upon itself) discovers the truth about the objects or things in the world. The first activity of sense-perception notices objects as independent of each other, as having no essential relations. Reflection, or attention in its higher powers, discovers necessary relations, and forms more adequate ideas of the truth. Isaac Newton saw the sun and planets as one gravitating whole—a *system*—and his knowledge certainly came nearer the truth than did the knowledge of previous astronomers who merely knew the sun and planets in their separate existence. In going into the truth of objects the mind goes into itself at the same time. Thus psychology points backward to the great fact that reason made the world as well as the human intellect.]

§ 83. Attention (depending as it does upon the voluntary powers of the mind) can be developed or educated. [The fact that the child is capable of exercising his will-power on his intellect is the fundamental fact that makes all intellectual education possible. There is no intellect, strictly speaking, until the will has combined with the perception.]

§ 84. (Note what has been said above in § 82). Perception, conception, and thinking are named as the three stages of intellect. [Perception (German word, *Anschauen*) here refers simply to the contemplation of objects by the senses. Conception (German word, *Vorstellen*) makes in the mind a picture of the object, but a *general* picture—a representation of the object in its outlines—a representation that will correspond not only to the particular object, but to all objects of the same class. Thinking perceives the essential relations of the object, its dependencies on its environment, and the reciprocal action. Education produces in the pupil the ability to carry back the activity of the higher faculties into the lower ones, as stated in the text. In the presence of perception the mind learns to be able to recall the general representation of the type or class of objects, and compare the object before the senses with the general type. It enables it also to think in the presence of the object, and to perceive essential relations at the same time that it is occupied with perception and conception. Thus it elevates the lower faculties to thinking perception and to thinking conception. The child delights in fairy tales because they play with the fixed conditions of actuality, and present to him a picture of free power over nature and circumstances. Thus they, to some extent, prefigure to him the conquest which his race has accomplished, and is accomplishing, only it is made to appear as the exploits of some Aladdin, or Jack the Giant Killer. To modify, change, or destroy "the limits of common actuality" is the perpetual work of the race. It molds the external world to suit its own ideas. Play is the first education that the child gets to prepare him for this human destiny.]

§ 85. Perception can be assisted by isolation of the object to be perceived. The pupil should be trained to look for certain properties and attributes, and to note their peculiarities. The categories under which one may classify these properties and attributes are furnished by reflection. Hence, when one in the so-called "object-lessons" trains the pupil to note in all objects certain constantly recurring predicates, such as color, shape, frangibility, solubility, size, number, taste, smell, etc., he is bringing thought and conception "back into perception" (see previous section) and elevating mere perception into *thinking* perception. The difference between ordinary perception and scientific perception lies just here: the former is unsystematic and fragmentary, the latter is systematic and exhaustive. Thinking gives the system. Hence, the training of perception is the subordination of it to the will, and the introduction of complete systematic habits of activity in place of accidental perception.]

§ 86. All perceivable objects should be learned by actual perception so far as is possible. When remoteness in space and time or inaccessibility on account of size prevents this, a good substitute offers itself in the way of pictorial representation. [The picture, of course, idealizes much—it magnifies some objects and reduces others, and it never presents all of the features found in nature. But it omits unessential details for the most part, and this fact makes a picture much easier to learn than the real object, although the knowledge is not so practical. The picture is commonly nearer the *type* or general form of the object than real specimens; the real specimens have much about them that is accidental, and need much comparison to discover what is the normal type. The picture gives this type at once, and hence gives assistance to the pupil—half digests his mental food for him, in fact. Hence the pictorial representation has advantages (easy of apprehension because it is a perception reduced to conception) and disadvantages (because the pupil does not get the strength that comes from reducing the specimens of nature to their types by his own efforts).]

§ 87. Accuracy is, above all, demanded in pictorial representations. The picture-book came into use chiefly after decline of painting. Comenius (1658) gave a great impulse to education by his book, which attempts to convey a knowledge of the world by pictures.

§ 88. Children should be exercised in classification. They should collect and arrange cabinets for themselves. [This will give them ability in recognizing the type in the specimen, the general in the particular. Drawing, too, is excellent practice, if from objects direct, inasmuch as it requires the pupil to omit all that is not characteristic of the object. How far lines suffice to delineate an object, and fix it unmistakably, and what these few lines are, the art of drawing teaches. Characterization must be learned first before any attempt at æsthetic effect. But true works of art must be placed where the child will receive a silent education from them, although no positive instruction is given in them.]

§ 89. Pictorial representation is of little service, unless accompanied by analysis and explanation. [Mere gazing upon a picture is like the thoughtless gazing upon real objects—it is not systematic, and does not separate the essential from the accidental, nor exhaust the subject.]

§ 90. Training of the ear by music and by correct speaking. [Tones are of all kinds—solemn, joyous, lively, sad, contemplative, discordant and suggestive of hate and bitterness, harmonious and sweet and suggestive of love and agreement, etc. There is a long scale of degrees to each one of these feelings and passions, and music can present all shades of each. Even the keys have each a special character. The German composers have used these and other properties of tones to advantage in constructing great musical dramas, in which pure music accomplishes results similar to words in poetry.]

§ 91. (1) Verification of conceptions through comparison of the conception with the perception; (2) creative imagination, which modifies or combines images; (3) memory, which holds fast perceptions by attaching them to arbitrary or conventional symbols, such as words.

§ 92. Method of verification and its function.

§ 93. [Emancipation of the mind takes place through its ascent into formative power, and this is realized in two ways: (a) in reaching the general types of objects, the mind finds the one form that stands for many, and gains ability to see the one in the many, the power to hold the essential and permanent without depending on any one particular object or specimen or sense-perception; (b) in reproducing, by aid of the general conception or abstract definition, a number of special examples, it is able to fashion them in various ways, and yet endow them all with possible attributes and characteristics. The mind thus has free scope of realization, and can, in an ideal world of its own creation, participate in creative activity.]

§ 94. In the epoch of the development of the imagination comes in the study of art and literature.

The first classics for youth are those which have been developed by nations in their earliest stages. Not only the light sides, but the darker sides of character in these *naïve* stories, are essential to their educative effect. They furnish types of human character, and types of human situations, a knowledge of which constitutes wisdom. The conception of the characters of Cain, Joseph, Samson, David, Saul, Ulysses, Penelope, Achilles, and the like, furnishes a ready classification for special objects of experience.

§ 95. Every child should read as indispensable the stock of stories which furnish these general types of character and situation. ["Robinson Crusoe," "Gulliver's Travels," "Don Quixote," the "Arabian Nights," the dramas of Shakespeare, should be read sooner or later. Earlier than these, the old English stories and fairy tales, and even Mother Goose's melodies. A scale thus extending from the earth to the fixed stars of genius furnishes pictures of human life of all degrees of concreteness. The meager and abstract outline is given in the nursery tale, and the deep comprehensive grasp of the situation with all of its motives is found in Shakespeare. The summation of the events of life in "Solomon Grundy" has been compared to the epitome furnished by Shakespeare in the "Seven Ages," and the disastrous voyage of the "Three Men of Gotham" is made a universal type of human disaster arising from rash adventure.]

§ 96. Importance of avoiding morbid tendencies in the stories for children. They must be *naïve* and not sentimental; but mere childishness is to be avoided.

§ 97. Earnestness must predominate over play, as the child advances into youth and youth into riper age. The biographies of Plutarch present well-executed pictures of men of colossal characters placed in difficult situations. Philosophical works, if taken up in later youth, should be classical treatises on special problems of thought. Abstracts and summaries are generally to be avoided.

§ 98. Memory. [The German word *Gedaechtniss* is contrasted with the word *Erinnerung*; the former may be translated "Memory," and the latter "Recollection"—Recollection, the reproduction of the perceived object in its particular existence, and Memory the reproduction of it by its general type. With the general type the mind is able to master the infinite diversity of nature and reduce all to a few classes. Mnemonic artifices are to be eschewed. "Memory is the stage of the dissolution of the conception;" this means that the power of representation becomes less and less, a mere recalling of what has been perceived, and, as the mind strengthens, it passes over into a faculty which calls up universals, or general concepts in the place of particular images. Memory, in this technical sense, deals with words—each word standing for some universal concept. Language is therefore something that can be used by a whole people—its words, standing, as they do, for universals, express for each individual the contents of his observations, no matter how peculiar they may be.]

§ 99. Repetition and the writing down of names and numbers are the best means for fixing them in the memory.

§ 100. In the general images of the faculty of conception, necessity of connection is yet wanting. Thinking, technically so called, discovers necessary relations.

§ 101. A sense of truth may be fostered from childhood up. Prejudice and self-interest must be habitually set aside for the truth—for the perception of things as they actually are. Great care, therefore, must be exercised to prevent illusions (the activity of the productive imagination, however essential it may be) from weakening the sense of truth.

§ 102. An acquaintance with logical forms is important for the thorough education of the intellect. Logical forms give the archetypes or simplest shapes of all problems that occur elsewhere. Neither mathematics nor any other application of logic in the sciences can supply the place of a logical training.

9 789361 387951

Printed by Libri Plureos GmbH in Hamburg,
Germany